Military Strategy & Sword Fighting

# Way of the Sword

A CLOSER LOOK AT THE SWORD SCROLL
VOLUME 1 OF 4

YAMAMOTO KANSUKE

TRANSLATION BY ERIC SHAHAN

ISBN: 978-1-950959-24-2

***Military Strategy & Sword Fighting : Way of the Sword***
**A Closer Look at the Sword Scroll Volume 1 of 4**
**Translator's Introduction**

Several years ago I completed a project about the 16th century Samurai Yamamoto Kansuke (1493-1561). The book, called *The Sword Scroll*, examined four sword fighting manuals attributed to him. These works, which were all published in the Edo Era, 1600-1868, explain Yamamoto Kansuke's sword, spear, hidden weapon and military strategy. While quite similar, each of the four editions of Kansuke's teachings in *The Sword Scroll* contained different illustrations and had other additions both major and minor. The purpose of *The Sword Scroll* was to remove any duplication of material within the four different versions and compile a single volume with all the information. This however, doesn't allow each book to stand on its own, so I have decided to re-format each edition into a stand-alone volume. This is the purpose of the four-part *A Closer Look at the Sword Scroll* series.

**About the Author**

Yamamoto Toki "Way of the Devil" Kansuke was a hero of the century long Sengoku Era, roughly 1467-1600. Though partially blind and lame in one leg, Yamamoto Kansuke's prowess as a military strategist was legendary and his methods became the subject of study.

Each of the four editions used in *A Closer Look at the Sword Scroll*, is actually a combination of two short works.

- 軍法兵法記釼術之巻 Gunpo Hyohoki Kenjutsu no Maki
  *Military Strategy and Sword Fighting The Sword Scroll*

- 軍法兵法記・奥義の巻 Gunpo Hyohoki O-gi no Maki
  *Military Strategy and Sword Fighting the Inner Secrets Scroll*

While identical in parts, each book contains interesting variations that collectively add a great deal of information to those interested in traditional Japanese martial arts and military strategy.

## Overview of the *A Closer Look at the Sword Scroll* series:

Volume 1

- **軍法兵法記釼術之巻 Gunpo Hyohoki Kenjutsu no Maki**
  ***Military Strategy and Sword Fighting Way of the Sword***
  Published after 1546
  The earliest version of these works with silhouette style illustrations.

Volume 2

- **剣道獨稽古 Kendo Hitori Geiko**
  ***An Illustrated Guide to Kendo Solo Training***
  19th century
  Notable for its excellent illustrations of early Kendo armor as well as the use of Tengu, mythical winged mountain goblins.

Volume 3

- **武術早學 Bujutsu Haya Manabi**
  **A Quick Guide to Martial Arts**
  **19th Century**
  This edition is notable for two additional sections showing boxing and wood staff techniques, which do not appear in any other version.

Volume 4

- **軍事参考軍法兵法記：楠正成秘書**
  **Kusonogi Masashige Hissho Gunji Sanko Gunpo Heiho Ki**
  ***Kusonogi Masashige's Secret Martial Arts Scroll on Military Strategy and Sword Fighting*** 1914
  This version contains commentary by researcher Wakichi Sakurai has a definitive publication date of. Sakurai draws parallels between Yamamoto Kansuke and the 14th century warlord Kusunoki Masashige 楠木正成 (1294 –1336.) He is held up as the ideal Samurai for his service to his lord.

## Outline of Yamamoto Kansuke's Life

Yamamoto Kansuke getting his eye gouged out by a wild boar whilst hunting.
*Yamamoto Kansuke Gunpaiden*山本勘助軍配團 18th century

Yamamoto Kansuke (1493-1561) whose given name is variously written as 勘助、勘介 or 菅助 was born at the end of the late 15th or early 16th century and died at the fourth Kawanakajima battle in 1561. His woodpecker strategy, similar to the pincer movement, was widely praised as an example of excellent military tactics. Unfortunately he believed his woodpecker strategy to be a failure so he attempted to regain his honor by charging into the enemy ranks, being killed in action.

His military strategy was first recorded in a chapter of the *Koyo Gunkan* 甲陽軍鑑 a 20 volume record of military strategy commissioned by the warlord Takeda Shingen. The oldest copy is from 1656.

## Translator's Note : Layout

Each page in this book has pictures of two combatants, as shown above. They are shown in different Stance, or stances, divided into three broad categories Jodan, Chudan and Gedan. Jodan is with the sword or spear held at or above head level, Chudan is around waist level and Gedan has the handle of the sword at waist level with the point facing the ground.

In addtion to the broad category of Jodan, Chudan and Gedan there is a sub-name for each illustration and a notation about foot positioning. The sub-names are quite poetic and therefore hard to translate accurately without being directly involved in this school of martial arts, therefore the translations should be considered approxamate. The notation regarding foot postitioning is either "floating foot" or "planted foot" which, based on the illustrations indicates the "ball of your foot off the ground" for the former and "foot flat on the ground" in the latter. It Some of the illustrations also contain additional information of varying lenghts.

For the most part each page will be presented as it was in the orininal book then each Stance will be isolated and enlarged, with the information on the page translated above. This is shown on the following page.

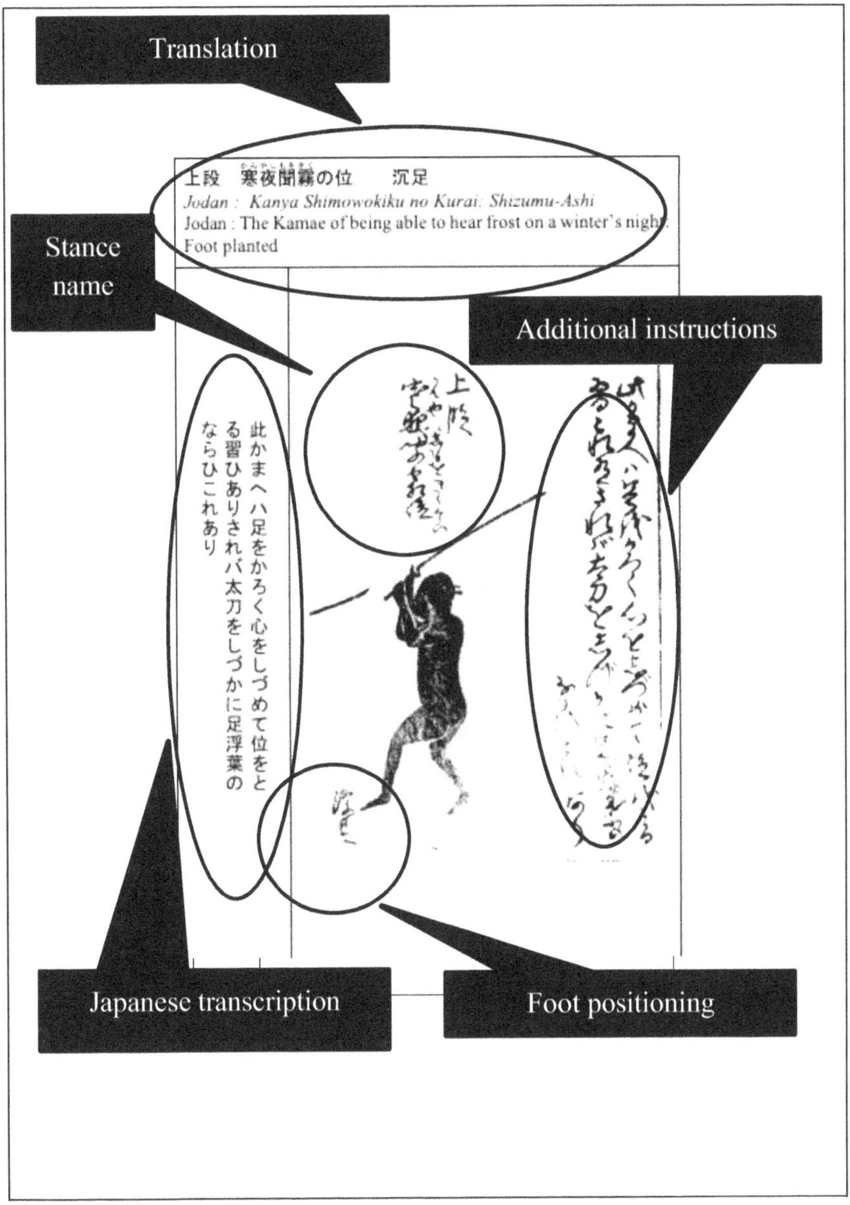
Translation
上段　寒夜聞霜の位　　沉足
Jodan : Kanya Shimowokiku no Kurai: Shizumu-Ashi
Jodan : The Kamae of being able to hear frost on a winter's night:
Foot planted
Stance name
Additional instructions
此かまへハ足をかろく心をしづめて位をと
る習ひありされバ太刀をしづかに足浮葉の
ならひこれあり
Japanese transcription
Foot positioning

此一巻君の命下守るが為に摘ミ以て幼雅の
時より弓馬にみちをうちたやらん事併のさき矢の
根代みかいて敵し闘ん事をおもふ故に書を綴る
なりして文の好悪を去るまで学びなさで行ば勇の名を
見たまへできるに今此書を君のひろんと秘宜
不成と申して御前の首尾を頼みてまつる者也

天文十五年 丙午
五月吉日

山本勘助 在判

長坂長閑老
御披露

# 軍法兵法記釼術之巻

**Gunpo Hyohoki Kenjutsu no Maki**

***Military Strategy and Sword Fighting : Way of the Sword***

As the life of your lord is of the upmost importance, I have crafted this scroll. From a young age I recall being enthralled with horse-riding and often thought of fighting enemies while polishing the shafts of arrows. For this reason when reading a document I do not dwell on whether or not the writing is good or lacking but if it instills a sense of bravery in me. Further, you should endeavor to become the kind of subject that uses such knowledge to serve your lord without shame and to complete all tasks assigned to you successfully and without fail.

Fifteenth year of Tenbun May First 1546
Yamamoto Dokisai (Dokisai is his Buddhist name) Kansuke
Haruyuki

Introduction by the revered elder
Nagasaka Chokan (?－1582)

目録

壱 剣術三ツの要といふ事

弐 上中下段かまへの太刀

三 さんきおふあんかまへの太刀

四 両刀をつかふ乃てだて

五 鑓長刀戦ひかまへのてだて

六 弓鉄砲たゝかひかまへの分式

七 入身の事

十 捕手の事

十二 早縄の事

十三 兵法者小心得有る事

九 居合の事

十四 忍者夜川虚実の事

十六 兵の太刀秘術の事

軍法兵法書

八 遁げ者仕留る事

十一 がんぜきくずきといふ事

十五 柔術あて身の事

十七 眼つぶしといふ事

敵二人我一人仕合の事

敵一人味方多勢仕合の事

川中仕合の事

家内仕合の事

日中仕合の事

月夜仕合の事

室の仕合の事

敵我後に来るべく事

敵の数色数持たる事

足場悪しき地にて仕合ふ事

## Table of Contents

# 軍法兵法記 剱術之巻

甲州住人　山本勘助著

## 剱術三ッの要といふ事

夫剱術に三ッの要あり 一ハ心 二ハ眼 三ハ手足なり 此三ッのものゝ相応する時ハ勝 違する時ハ負るなり 心ハ眼に随ひ 眼動眼に随ひて手足を動かすなり 此心逆ふ時ハ眼もちがひけれバ手足も手足眼にかなハざる時ハまけ 利やあらんとて三ッのものおなじくして慣れ熟れば利あるべし 是迄手の内に足のふみを修行あるべきべき事なり

## 上中下段構の事

それ剱術構ハ上段中段下段の三ッの外ハ無し是

# Gunpo Hyoho Kenjutsu no Maki
# 軍法兵法記釼術之巻
## 甲州住人山本勘助

***Military Strategy and Sword Fighting : The Way of the Sword***
**by Yamamoto Kansuke, Resident of Koshu**

### 劔術三ツの要いふ事
### The Three Essential Points of Kenjutsu

There are three basic principles in Kenjutsu. One is the spirit. The second is the eye. The third comprises the feet and hands. If these three are all in accordance/balance then you will achieve victory. If they are confused then you will be defeated. In accordance means that the spirit, the mind, is communicating to the eyes correctly. It means the eyes are correctly directing the feet and hands. In confusion means the eyes do not move in accordance with the spirit.

Having eyes delay the movement of the limbs of the body will give a poor result. However, if these three elements are activated correctly and in unison the result will be positive. This is exactly the same as the condition whereby having moved the hands you are not sure of where to put your feet.

絃術の秘事なり文字を唇とする事也食飽にしてよりしとき
わなへ手に附絃術は秘をしるべくその味を得るべし云々にして
得るあるといふゑんめり音にてしかし徵はめりきさ
まとらし云の要をかるはめりて書しとるその秘をたいふ
能は心得てあるといへとも委細しるよりて故に手覚乃
曲にて得てし是にあるし也

構様長刀は心得なり文上段の内に上中下乃
三つ段とも中段にも下段にも三段づゝあり
すなはち三十二あり擬術は千変万化して無窮なる
ものなり是は上中下の三段をおきて他は皆三段なり
よく合得て截り踏みを変に應じて對する事也

## 上中下段構の事
## Jodan, Chudan and Gedan Stances

When going into stances with a sword, know that Jodan, Chudan and Gedan are the only Kamae. This is the first lesson of Kenjutsu. Further, when studying and adapting your body to these Kamae having Yokoshimana Kokoro 邪な心 or no evil in your heart is best.

A person came to me once and said "In Kenjutsu the shape changes depending on the enemy. It follow then that there is only one Kimeru 極める, or only one rule, in Kenjutsu. What do you think of this?

The response was, "Having control over your spirit is certainly a Kimeru 極める. And having learned the three principals, or Kaname 要, you can consider yourself to have arrived, or Itaru 至る. Having achieved this state of Shigoku 至極, or the ultimate, there is really nothing more to be said. For that reason, the way in which the arms and legs are bent should be studied extensively.

For example, this applies in the same way to both Yari and Naginata. Further, within Jodan Kamae there lies Jo-upper, Chu-middle and Ge-lower. Also within Chudan Kamae there lies Jo-upper, Chu-middle and Ge-lower. All together there are thirty-three versions. It is said that Kenjutsu contains Sen-pen-ban-ka 千変万化 or a thousand changes and ten thousand variations, or Muryo or without end. However there are no other Kamae than Jodan, Chudan and Gedan. Those that are Shoshin Sha or beginners should study these three levels. Taking hold of any chance and responding to any Henka, or variation, by striking is of the upmost importance.

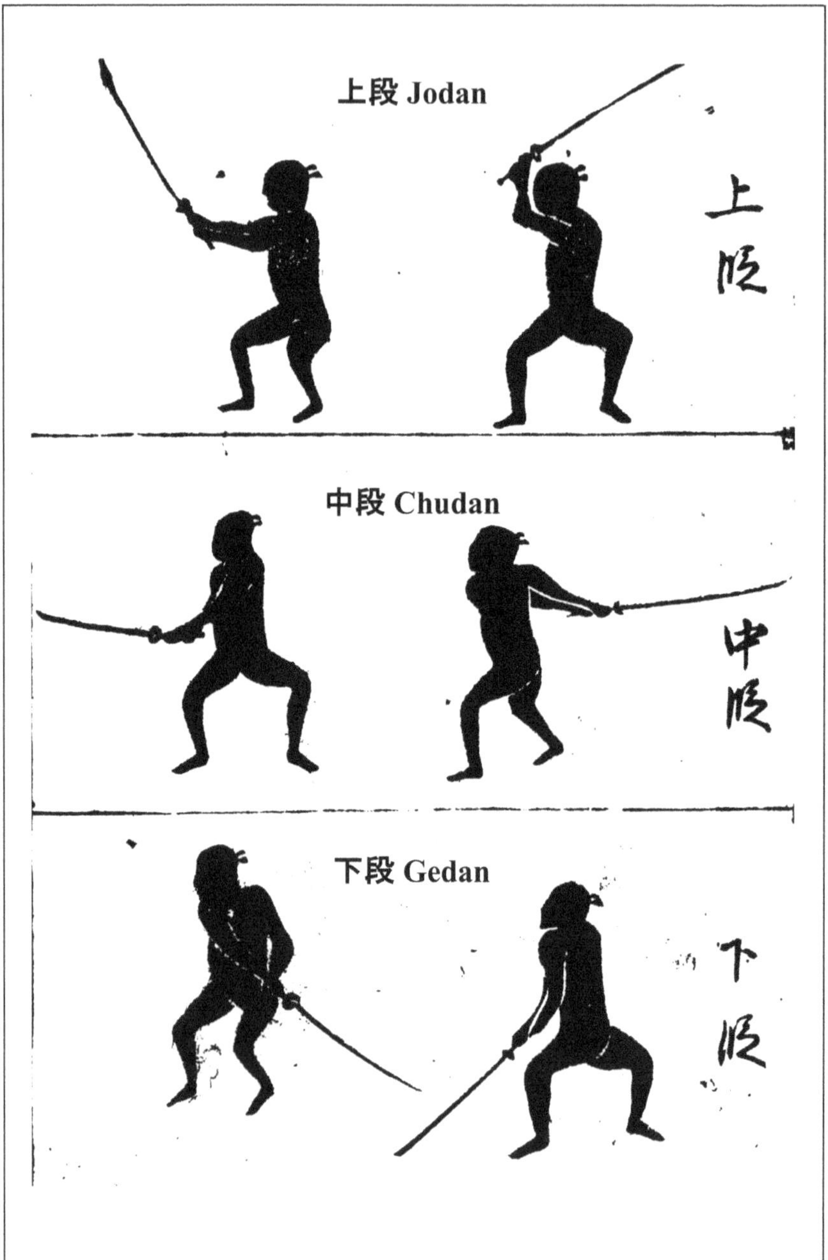
上段 Jodan
上段
中段 Chudan
中段
下段 Gedan
下段

上段
上段
上段
中段

## 上段電光（でんこう）の位　浮足

*Jodan : Denko no Kurai : Uki-ashi*

Jodan : Lightning Stance : Floating foot

This Kamae is about the Ma-ai 間合い or distancing of Irimi 入身, or entering into an ideal space in response to the opponent's attack or movement, and Hikimi 引身, or drawing back into an ideal position in response to the opponent's attack or movement. The foot is lightly touching the ground, the Tachi 太刀 is imbibed with the Denko Hiden, or the secret teaching of lightning.

上段電光（でんこう）の位　浮足

此かまえ入引の位これありされバ足をかろく、太刀に電光の習ひあり

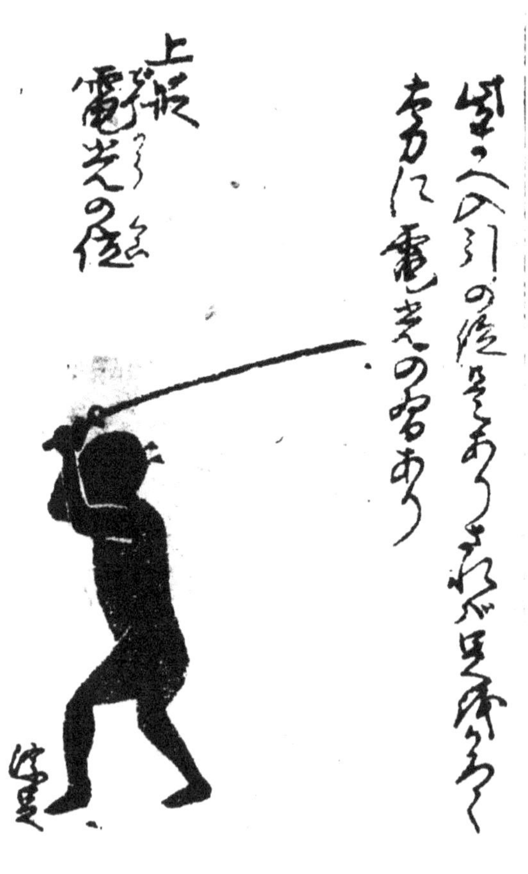

上段　寒夜聞霧（かんやしもをきく）の位　　浮足

*Jodan :  Kanya Shimowokiku no Kurai: Uki-Ashi*

Jodan : The Kamae of being able to hear frost on a winter's night: Floating Foot

此かまへハ足をかろく心をしづめて位をとる習ひありされバ太刀をしづかに足浮葉のならひこれあり

## 上段　寒夜聞霜の位　沉足

*Jodan : Kanya Shimowokiku no Kurai: Shizumu-Ashi*

Jodan : The stance of being able to hear frost crack on a winter's night : Planted foot

The secret teaching of this stance is to stay light on your feet and calm your spirit. Having done that draw the Tachi and position it silently. The feet should be kept as light as a leaf floating on water. The feet are of upmost importance.

此かまへに眼付けのならひあり敵の表裏におどろかず足をふみすえ心をしづめて位をとるべし

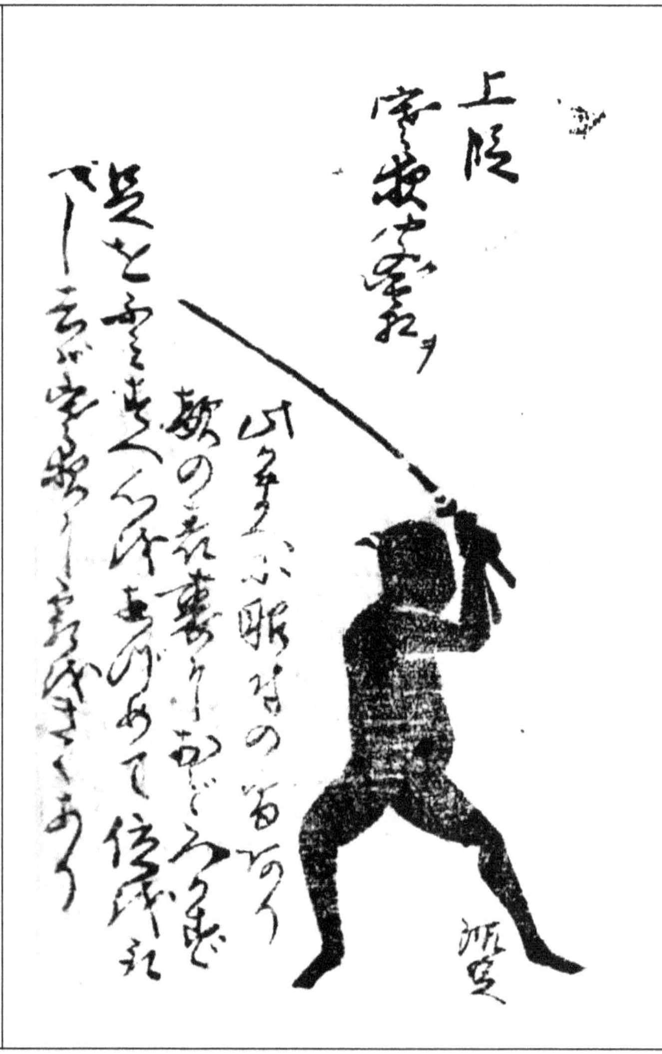

中段　一葉浮水（いちえふすい）の位　浮足

*Chudan : Ichi-e Fusui no Kurai : Uki-Ashi*

Chudan : Leaf floating upon water Stance:  Floating Foot

The meaning of this stance is to position yourself like a leaf floating upon water.  The feeling should be as if the feet are stepping on thin ice.

此かまへ浮水の習これあり足に薄氷（はくひょう）を
ふむこゝろあり

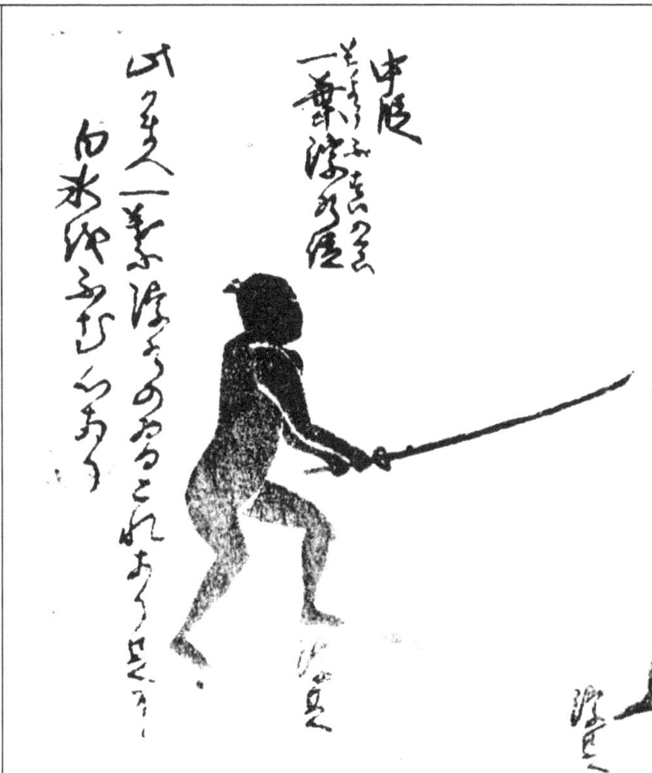

上段
中段
下段

### 上段　電光の位　沉足

*Jodan : Denko no Kurai : Shizumu-Ashi*

Jodan : Lightning Stance : Planted Foot

As you alternate switching your feet out your center of gravity moves back to front. For this stance you should concentrate on both what is in front of you as well as what is behind you. Your body should move lightly, dancing like a butterfly. If done in this fashion, from the opponent's point of view, it will seem to him as if you are in front of him when suddenly you have circled around behind him. Therefore you are extremely hard to corner. This is the stance known as Denko no Kurai, the Lightning Stance.

此かまへ前後に心をめぐらし身舞蝶の如くせよとなり
されば前にあるかとすればこつぜんとして後にあり
ゆえに電光の位といふ足ハこれりむさいをふむならひあり

**中段　浮船の位　浮足**

*Chudan Fusen no Kurai : Uki-Ashi*

Chudan : The Floating Boat Stance : Floating Foot.

The feeling of this stance is of watching the opponent's Tachi while you float like an object going up and down waves. That is why this Stance is called Fusen no Kurai, the Floating Boat Stance. The feet are touching lightly and the bodyweight should be placed as lightly as a feather.

此かまへ波にうかべるものゝごとく敵の太
刀にのるべき心ありされば浮船の位とい
ふ足をかろくふみ身をかうもりの如くせよ

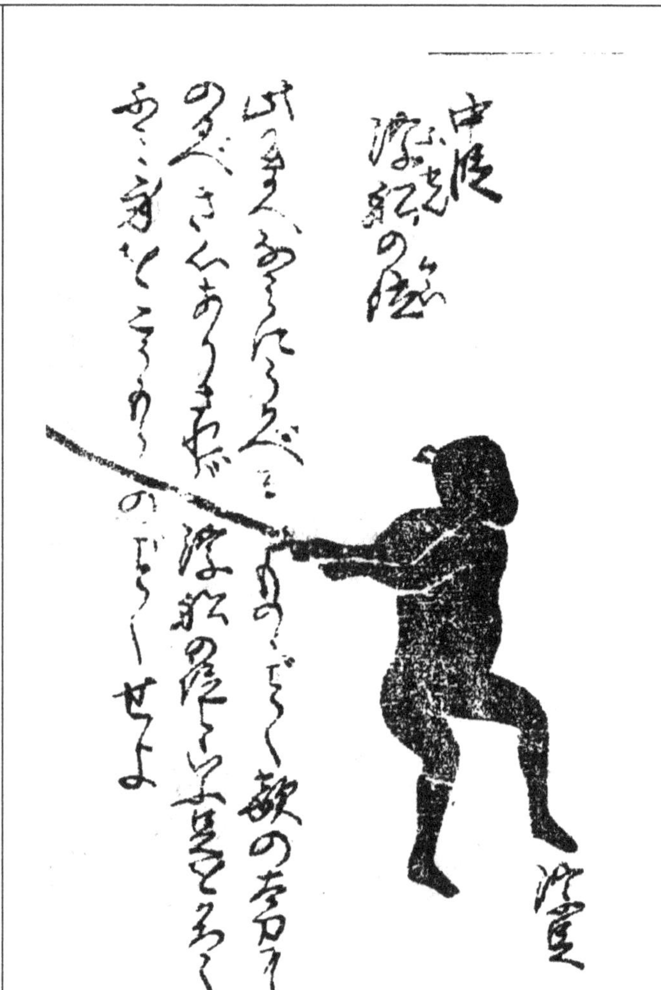

上段　村雲の位　沉足

*Jodan : Sonun no Kurai : Shizumu-Ashi*

Jodan : Cloudy Village Stance : Planted foot

Keep the feet together and impart a sense of sleepiness. The meaning of this stance is to clear your vision, calm your spirit and focus everything on the opponent's strategy. By doing this you will invariably discern something.

此かまへハ眼をすまし心をしづめて敵の手位
をみる事専一なり、必此内に一重のならひ有
之是を閑眼のおしへといふ

## 下段 村雲の位　浮足

*Gedan : Sonun no Kurai : Uki-Ashi*

Gedan : Cloudy Village Stance : Floating Foot

There is nothing in this stance that teaches that the spirit is in tumult. Like windblown clouds, across the face of the moon your spirit should be like a boat slowly being swept up onto the beach.

Note: The Kanji for Cloudy Village Stance are sometimes written as Sonun no Kurai and sometimes as Murakumo.

此かまへのうちに乱心のおしへ有、されバ風に雲の行ごとく雲ゆけば月もゆく船ゆけばきしもゆくといふ心なり

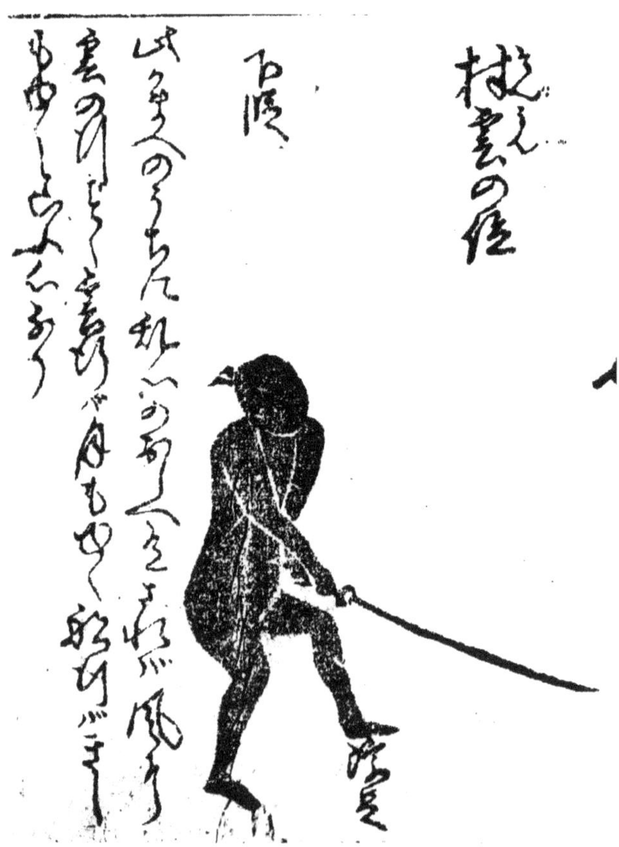

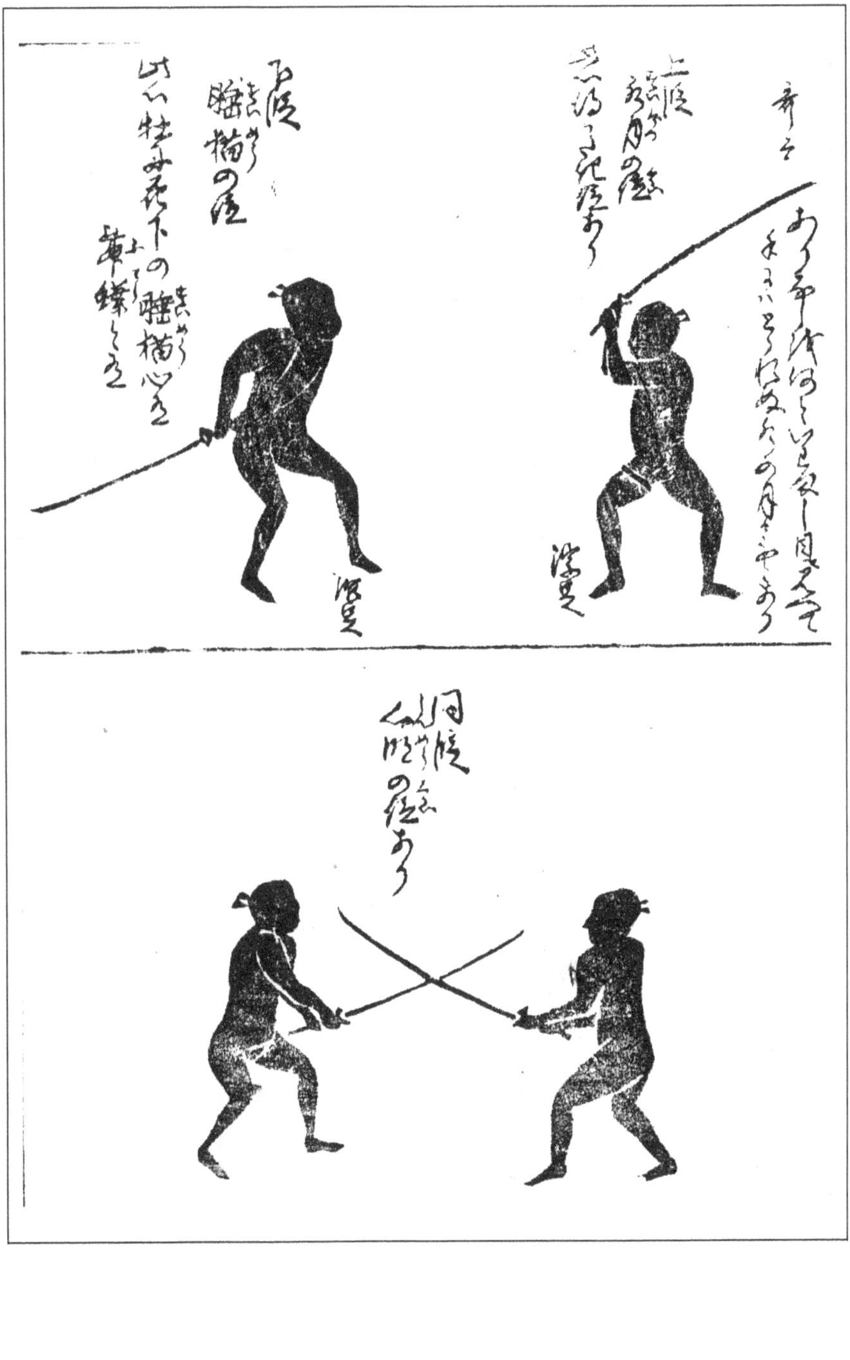

### 上段　水月の位　浮足

*Jodan : Suigetsu no Kurai : Uki-Ashi*

Jodan : Moon Reflected on Water Stance : Floating Foot

There is a song that talks of how this is a difficult stance to adopt. It is said that what is there is not there. The water that pools in one hand shows a different moon from the one above.

この心得かたき位なり歌に云う、ありなしを何といはまし月にミえて手にハしられぬ水の月かなとあり

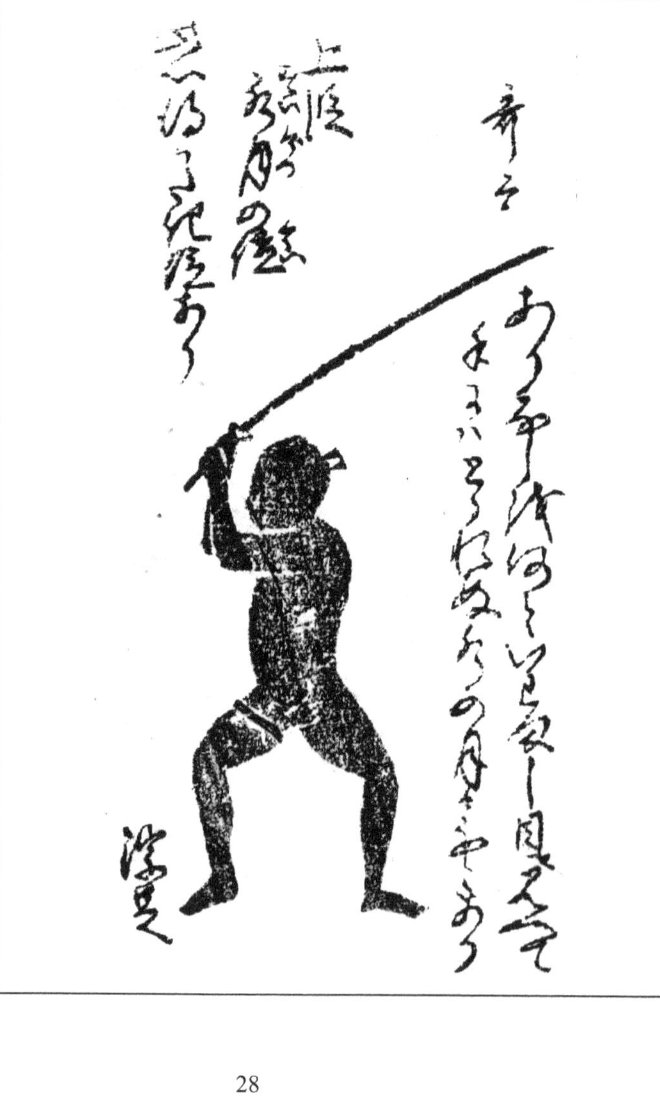

下段　睡猫(すいびょう)の位　沉足

*Gedan : Suibyou no Kurai : Shizumu-Ashi*

Gedan : Sleeping Cat Stance : Planted Foot

The way of thinking about this stance is a sleeping cat below a Botan flower with a dancing butterfly above.

この心牡丹花下(ぼたんかか)の睡猫心あり舞蝶とあり

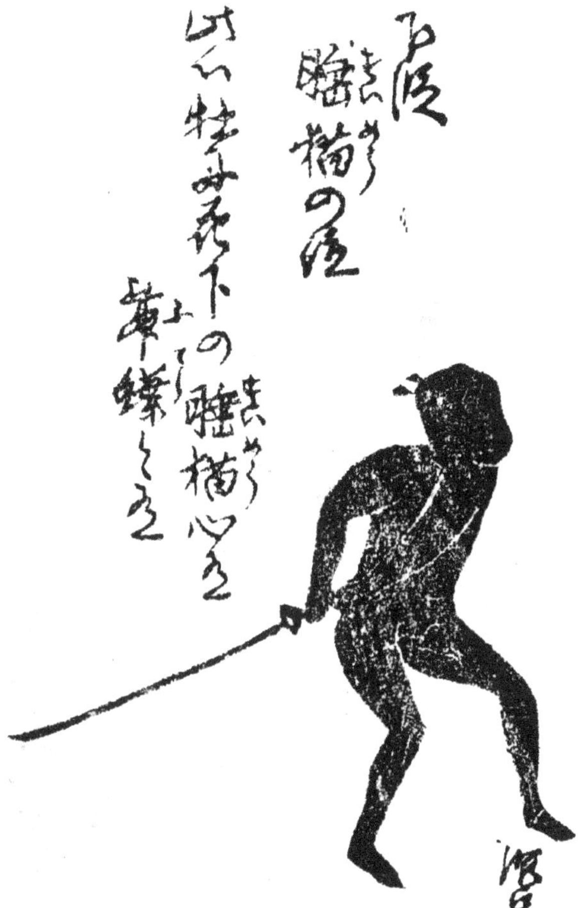

同段　　心妙の位あり
*Do-Stance : Shinmyo no Kurai*
Same Stance: Mysterious Heart Stance

There is a Kuden, Orally Transmitted Lesson

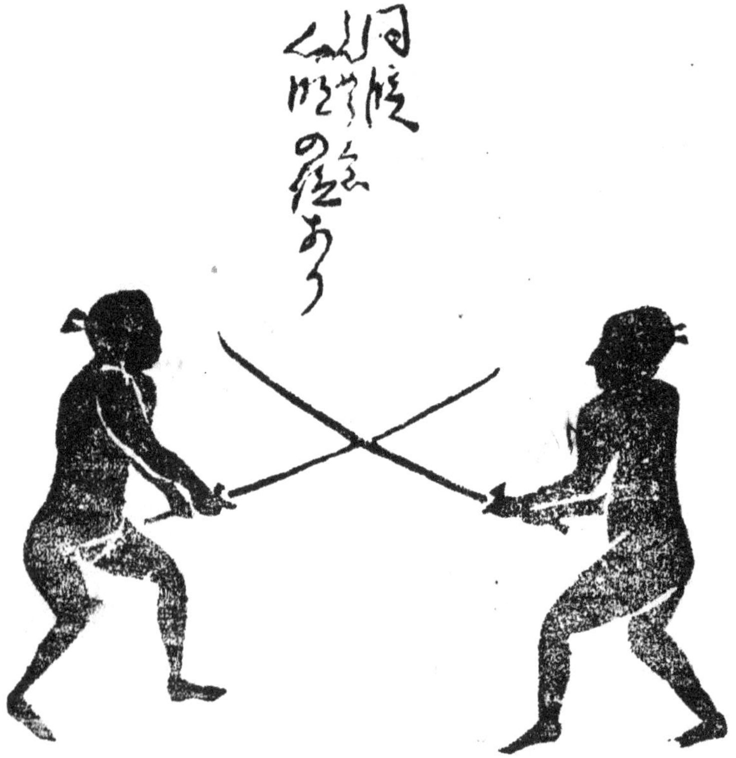

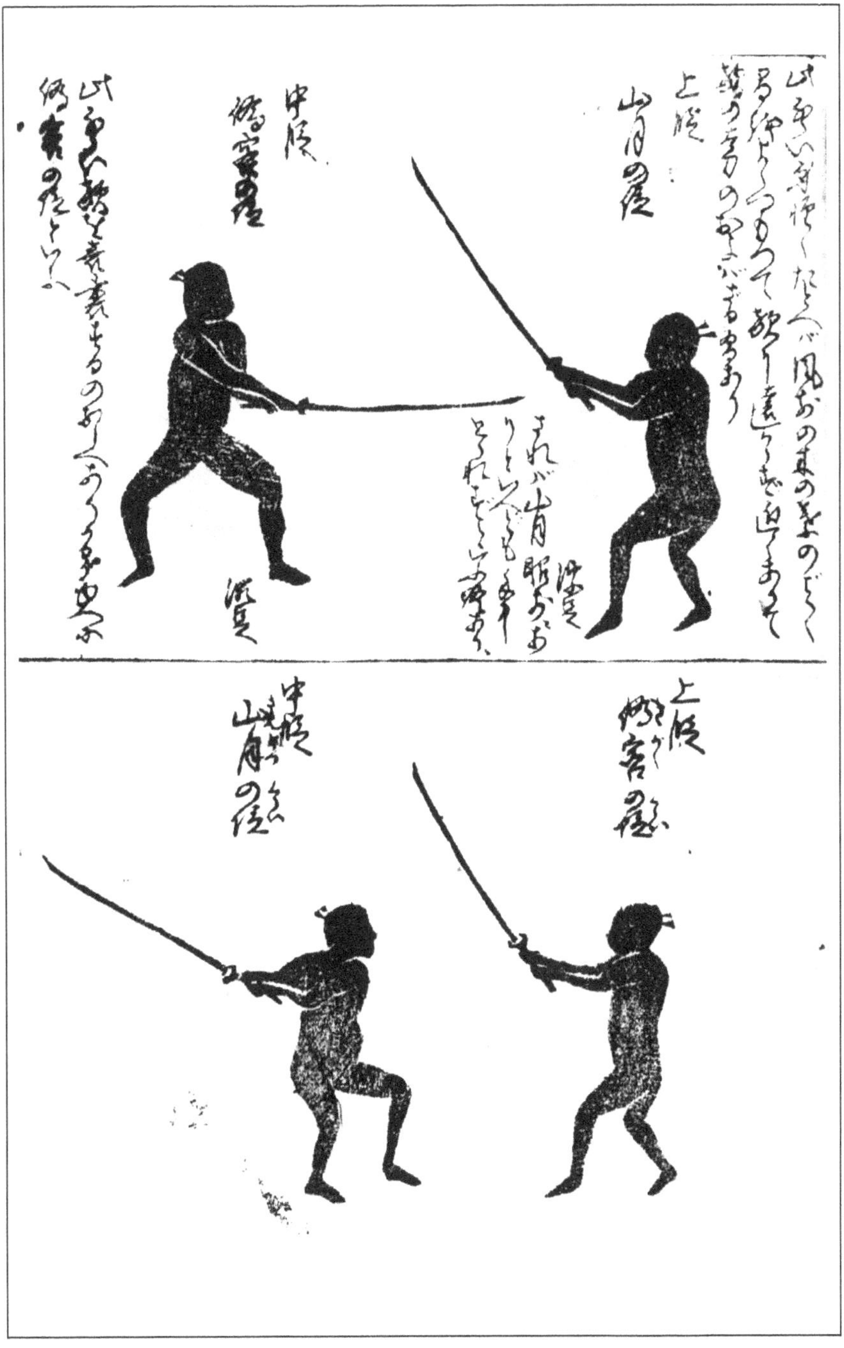

**上段　山月の位　浮足**

*Jodan : Sangetsu no Kurai : Uki-Ashi*

Jodan : Mountain Moon Stance : Floating Foot

For this Stance you should hold your body as light as a leaf on a tree being brushed by the wind. Maintain your Ma-ai, or distance, but do not allow the enemy too much space. Maintain a close distance but out of range of the enemy's Tachi. The meaning of this Stance is that while you can see mountains or the moon with your eyes you are unable to take them into your hand.

此ならひ身軽くたとへバ風前の木の葉の如く。間をよく
つもつて敵にからすくありて敵の太刀の及バざる習ひあり
されバ山月眼前にありといへども手にしられずといふ語あり

中段　偽客の位　　沉足
*Chudan : Gikaku no Kurai : Shizumu Ashi*
Chudan : False Guest Stance : Planted Foot

This Stance contains teachings on how to control the Hyori, or Obverse and Reverse, of the opponent. Both his true and hidden intent. For that reason it is known as Gikaku, False Guest.

此ならひ敵を表裏するのをしへありかるがゆえに偽客のくらいといふ

(Left) 中段山月の位 Chudan : *Sangetsu no Kurai*
Chudan : Mountain Moon Stance

(Right) 上段偽客の位 *Jodan* : *Gikaku no Kurai*
Jodan : False Guest Stance

**上段　清眼の位　浮足**

*Jodan Seigan no Kurai Uki-Ashi*

Jodan : Seigan Stance: Floating foot

Here you are meant to keep your eye on the end of the opponent's Tachi while at the same time keep your other eye on the eight directions around you.

眼を敵の太刀先につけ八面一眼といふ習あり
ことわりまへにあり

下段　睡猫（すいびょう）の位　沈足

*Gedan Suibyo no Kurai Shizumu-Ashi*

Gedan: Sleeping Cat Stance : Planted foot

Explanation is the same as before

寒夜聞霧の位　浮

*Kanyashimo wo Kiku no Kurai Uki-Ashi*

Floating foot : The stance of being able to hear frost crack on a winter's night : Floating Foot.

Note: I presume this is Jodan, however there is no notation.

入引の位　浮

ことわり電光の位に具（つぶさ）に書くしるし侯也

*Nyuin no Kurai Uki-Ashi*

Moving In and Out Stance :  Floating Foot

The explanation for this is the same as for Denko no Kurai.

Note: I presume this is Gedan, however there is no notation.

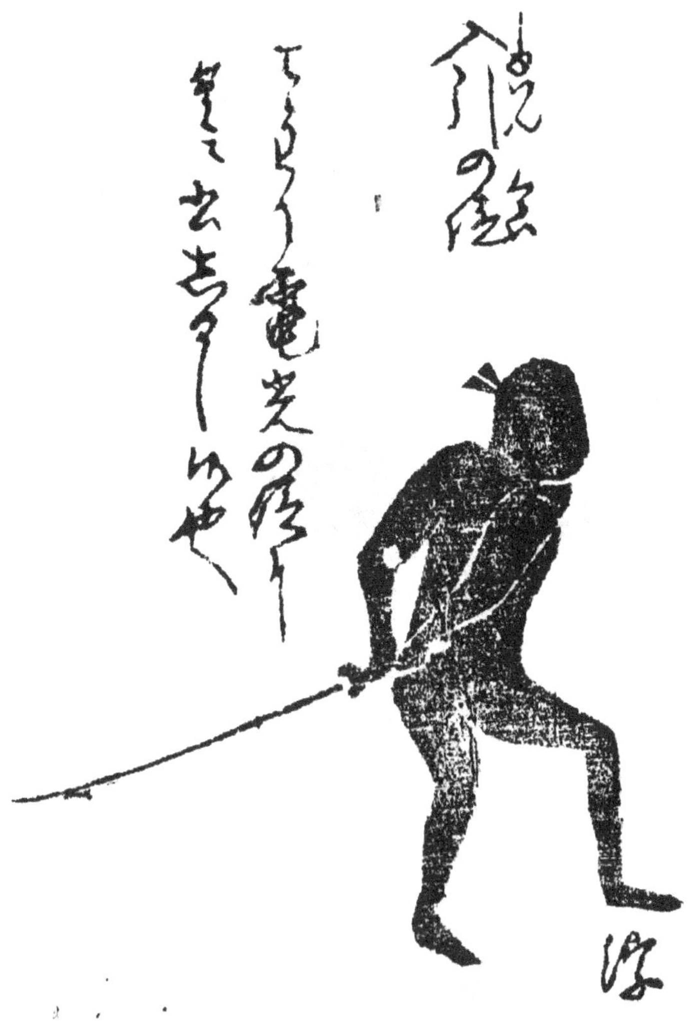

(Right) 中段 清眼の位 浮 *Chudan : Seigan no Kurai : Uki-Ashi* Chudan : Clear-eyed Stance : Floating foot
ことわりまへにあ Explanation is as before.

(Left) 下段 村雲の位 浮 *Gedan : Murakumo no Kurai : Uki-Ashi* Gedan: Cloudy Village Stance : Floating foot

(Right) 中段清眼の位浮足 *Chudan : Seigan no Kurai : Uki-Ashi* Chudan : Clear-eyed Stance : Floating foot
ことわりまへにあり Explanation is as before.

(Left) 下段　村雲の位浮足 *Gedan : Murakumo no Kurai Uki-Ashi Gedan* : Floating Foot

(Right) 中段 清眼の位 浮 *Chudan : Seigan no Kurai : Uki-Ashi*
Chudan : Clear-eyed Stance : Floating foot
ことわりまへにあ Explanation is as before.

(Left) 下段 村雲の位 浮 *Gedan : Murakumo no Kurai : Uki-Ashi*
Gedan: Cloudy Village Stance : Floating foot

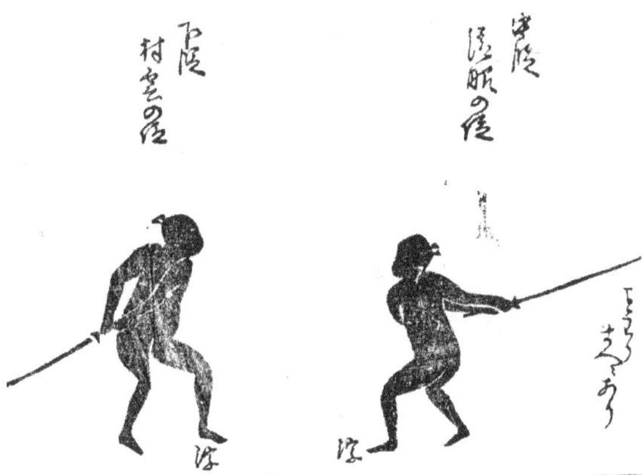

(Right) 中段清眼の位浮足 *Chudan : Seigan no Kurai : Uki-Ashi*
Chudan : Clear-eyed Stance : Floating foot
ことわりまへにあり Explanation is as before.

(Left) 下段 村雲の位浮足
Gedan : Murakumo no Kurai Gedan : Floating Foot

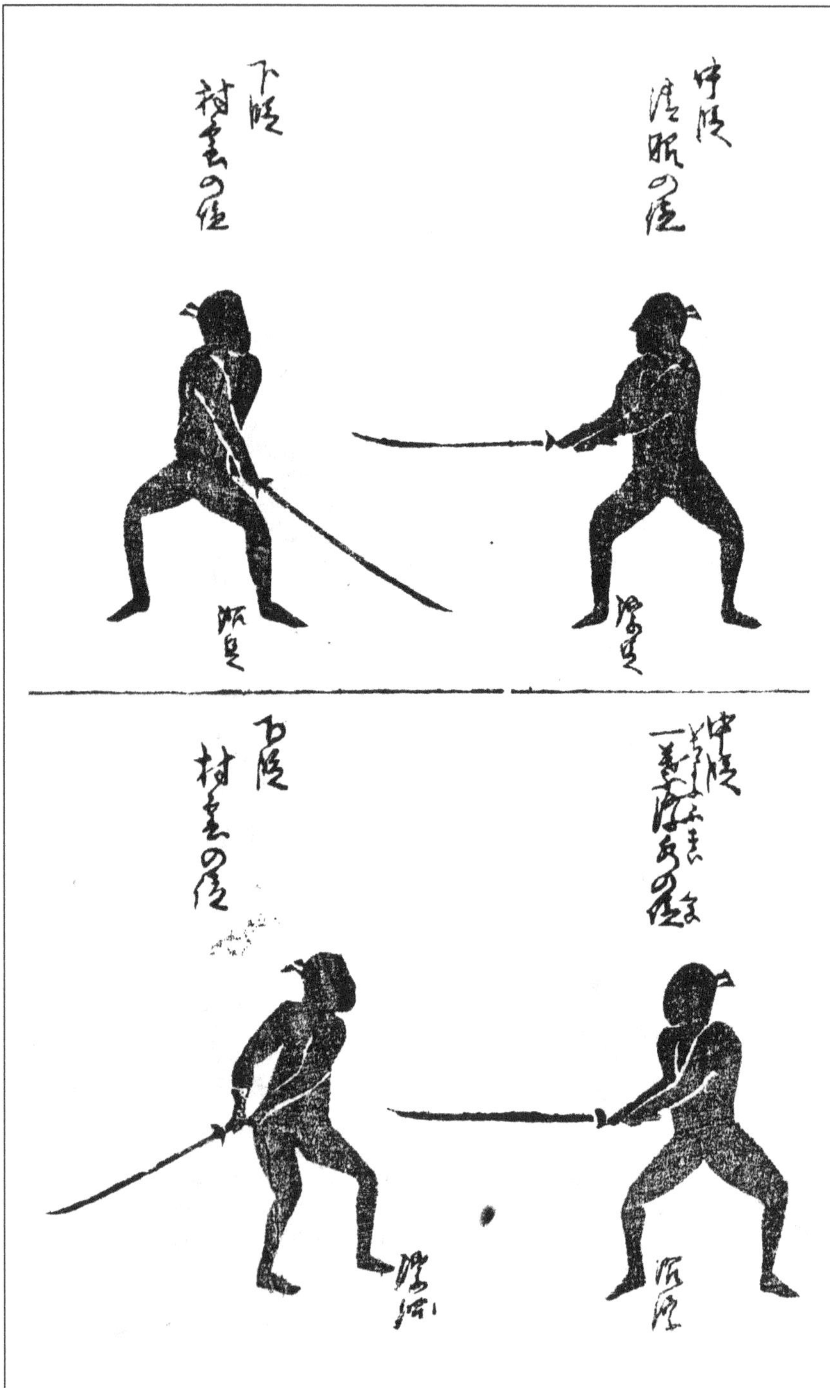

(Right)
中段 清眼の位浮足 *Chudan : Seigan no Kurai : Uki-Ashi*
Chudan : Clear-eyed Stance : Floating foot

(Left)
下段 村雲の位沉 *Gedan : Murakumo no Kurai :Shizumu-Ashi*
Gedan : Cloudy Village Stance : Planted foot

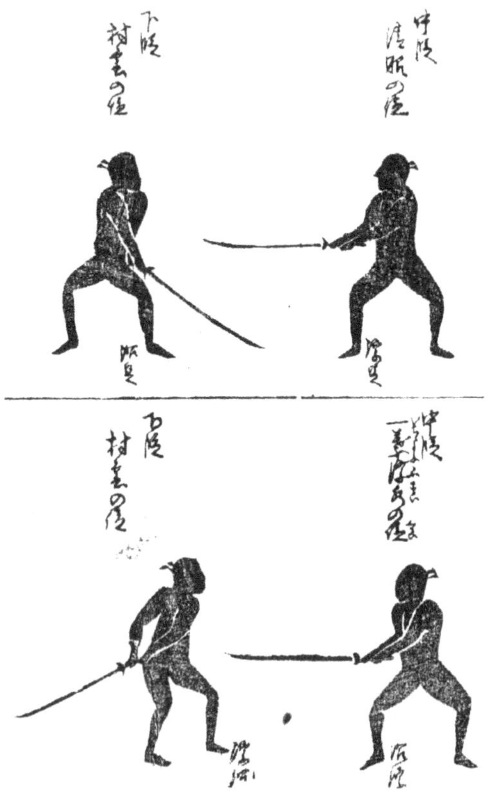

(Right)
中段 清眼の位沉 *Chudan : Seigan no Kurai : Shizumu-Ashi*
Chudan : Clear-eyed Stance : Planted Foot

(Left)
下段　村雲の位浮足 *Gedan : Murakumo no Kurai : Uki-Ashi*
Gedan : Cloudy Village Stance : Floating Foot

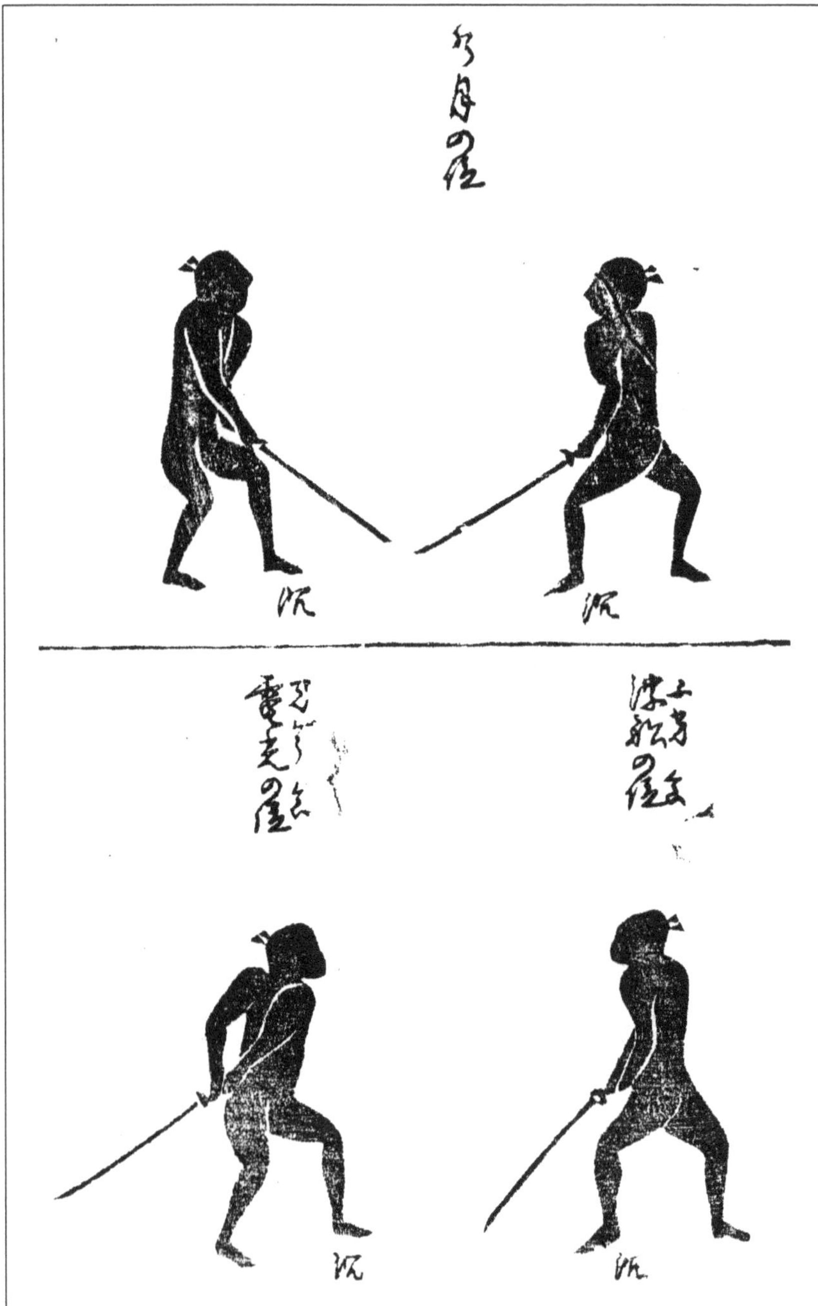

水月の位沈足 *Suigetsu no Kurai : Shizumu-Ashi*
Clear-eyed Stance : Planted Foot

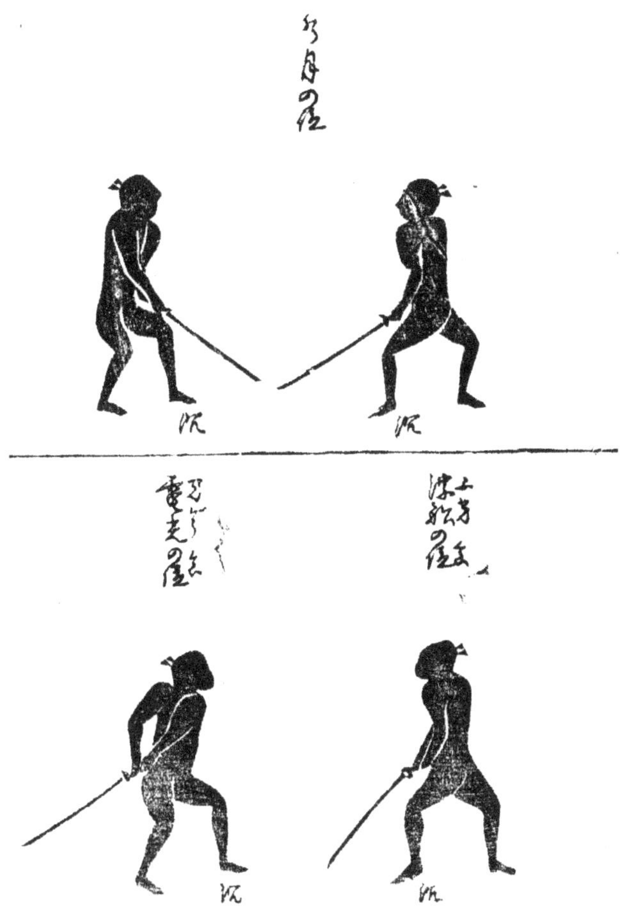

(Left)
電光の位沈足 *Denko no Kurai : Shizumu-Ashi*
Lightning Bolt Stance : Planted Foot

(Right)
ふ せん
浮船の位沈足 *Fusen no Kurai : Shizumu-Ashi*
Floating Boat Stance : Planted Foot

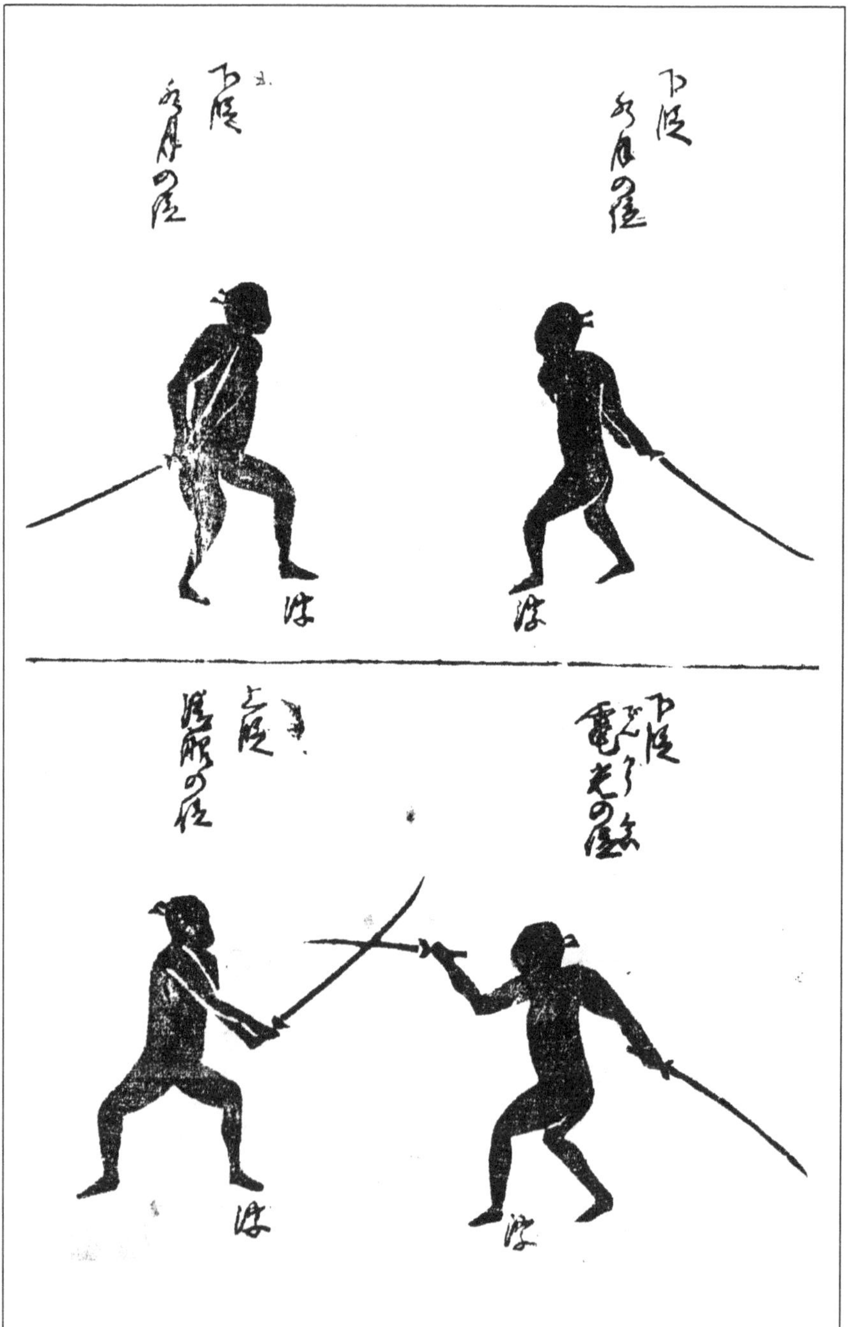
下段
下段
下段
電光の位
上段

(Left) 下段 水月の位 浮 *Gedan : Suigetsu no Kurai : Uki-Ashi*
Gedan : Moon Reflected on Water Stance: Floating foot

(Right)
下段 水月の位 浮 *Gedan : Suigetsu no Kurai : Uki-Ashi* Gedan : Moon Reflected on Water Stance : Floating foot

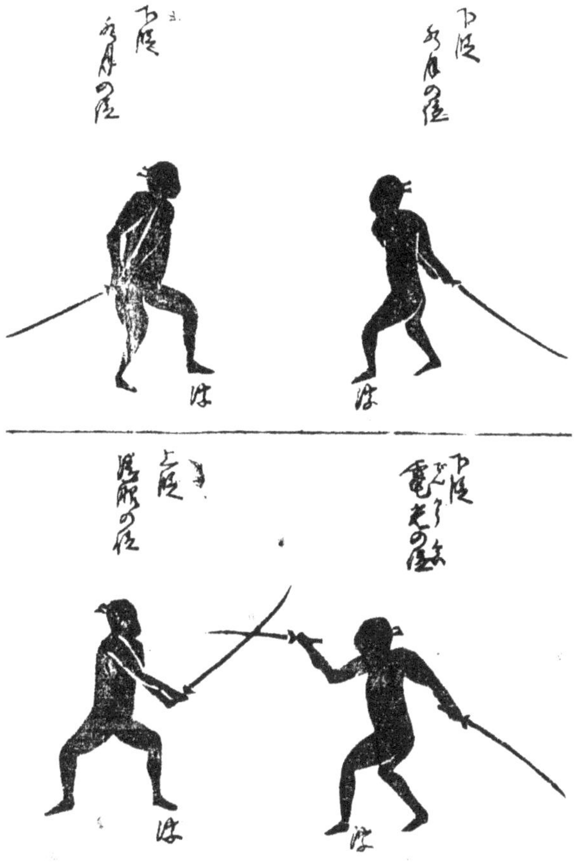

(Left)
下段 電光の位浮 *Gedan : Denko no Kurai : Uki-Ashi*
Gedan : Lightning Stance : Floating foot

(Right)
下段 清眼の位浮 *Gedan : Seigan no Kurai : Uki-Ashi*
Gedan : Clear-eyed : Floating foot

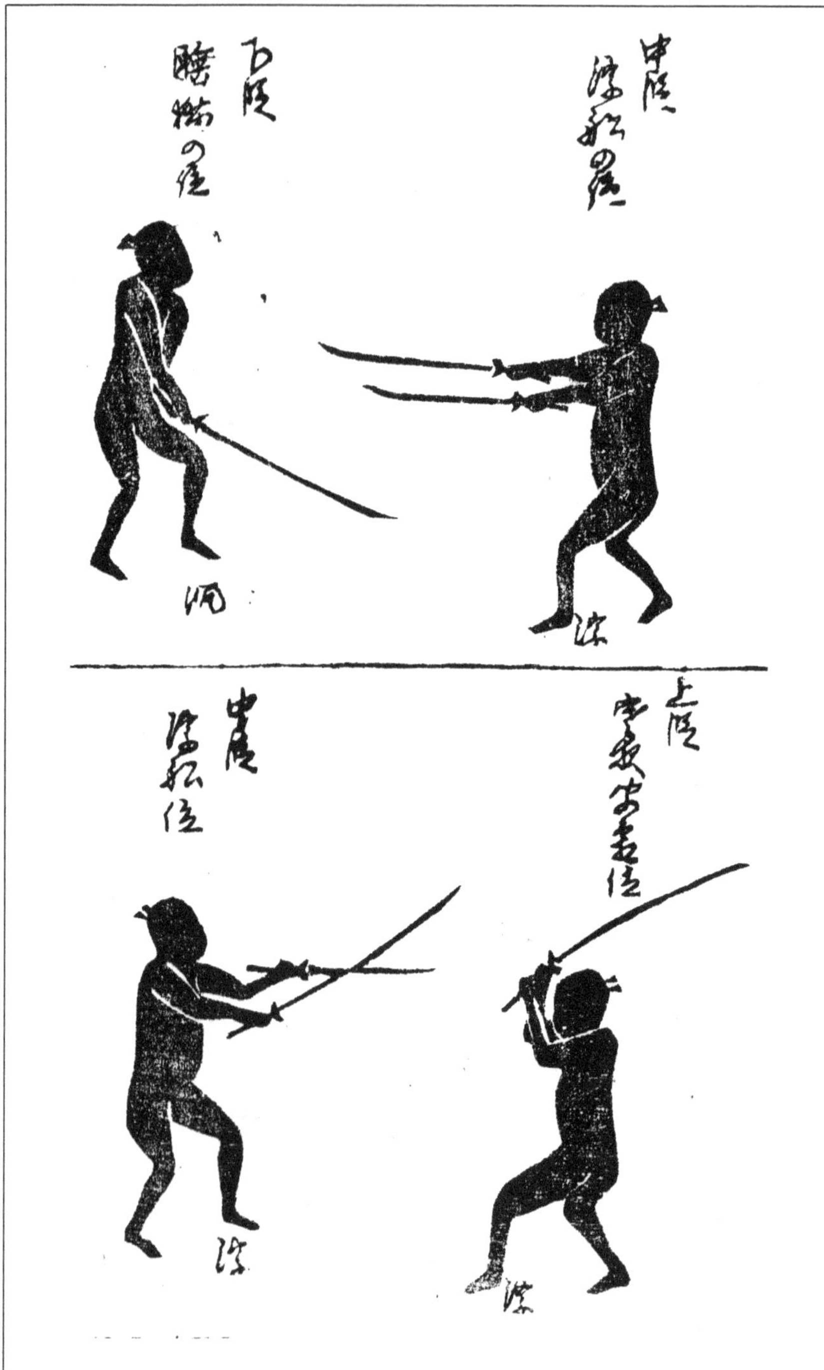

(Left) 下段 睡猫 *Gedan : Suibyo no Kurai Shizumu-Ashi*
Gedan : Sleeping Cat Stance : Planted Foot

(Right) 中段浮船の位 *Chudan : Ukibune no Kurai : Uki-Ashi*
Chudan : Floating Boat Stance : Floating Foot

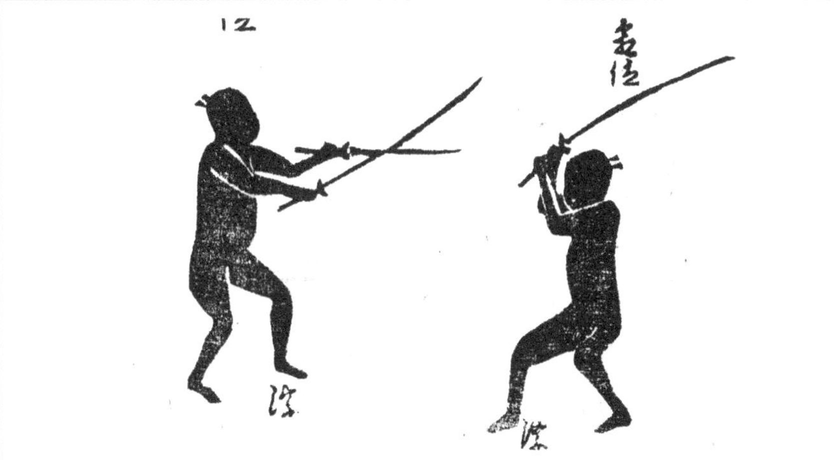


(Left) 中段浮船の位浮足 *Chudan : Ukibune no Kurai : Uki-Ashi*
Chudan : Floating Boat Stance : Floating Foot

かんやしもをきく
(Right) 上段寒夜聞霧の位浮足
*Jodan : Kanyashimo wo Kiku no Kurai : Uki-Ashi*
The stance of being able to hear frost crack on a winter's night : Floating Foot

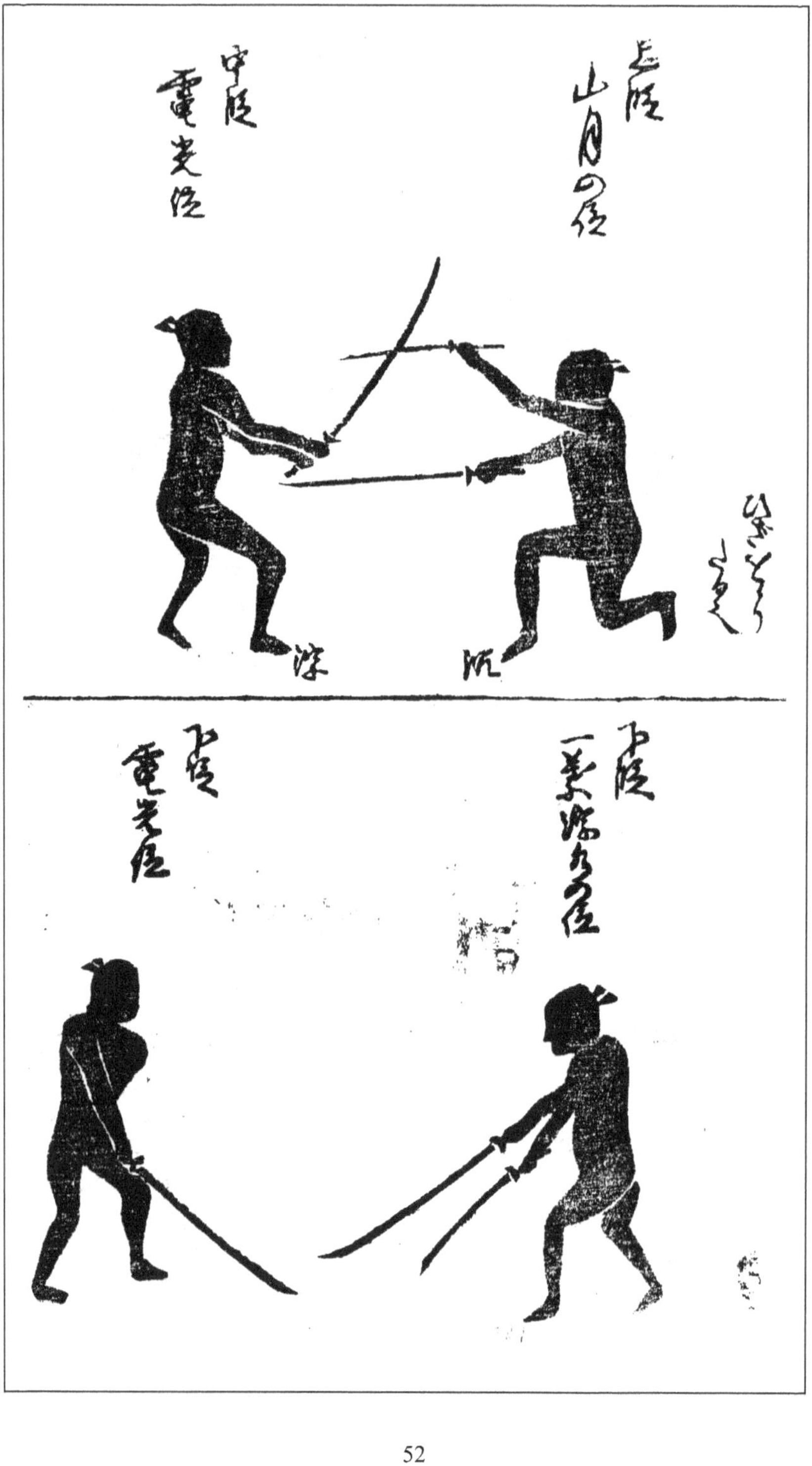
上段
山月の位
中段
電光位
下段
電光位
下段

(Left)
中段電光の位浮き *Chudan : Denko no Kurai : Uki-Ashi*
Chudan : Lightning Bolt Stance : Floating Foot

(Right)
上段　山月の位沈 *Jodan : Yamatsuki no Kurai : Shizumu-Ashi*
Jodan : Mountain Moon Stance : Planted Foot.
膝を付ける Plant the knee on the ground.

(Left)
下段電光の位 *Gedan : Denko no Kurai : Uki-Ashi*
Gedan : Lightning Bolt Stance : Floating Foot

(Right)
下段一葉浮水の位 *Gedan : Ichiefusui no Kurai : Shizumu-Ashi*
Gedan: Leaf floating upon water Stance : Planted Foot

上段
中段

(Left and right) 浮 Uki- Ashi : Floating foot
Note: The round ball on the end of the spear is padding for training.

(Left) 中段　寒夜聞霧（かんやしもをきく）の位沉
*Chudan : Kanyasimowokiku no Kurai : Shizumu-Ashi*
Chudan : The stance of being able to hear frost crack on a winter's night : Planted foot

(Right) 上段水月の位　浮沉
*Jodan Suigetsu no Kurai Uki-Shizumu Ashi*
Jodan : Moon Reflected on Water Stance : Floating/Planted Foot*
*The technique indicates both Floating and Planted are used.

Left)
上段 電光の位下段 浮沉
*Jodan: Denko no Kurai : Uki-Shizumu Ashi*
Jodan : Lightning Bolt Stance : Floating/Planted foot

(Right)
村雲の位　沉 *Murakumo no Kurai : Shizumu-Ashi*
Cloudy Village : Planted foot

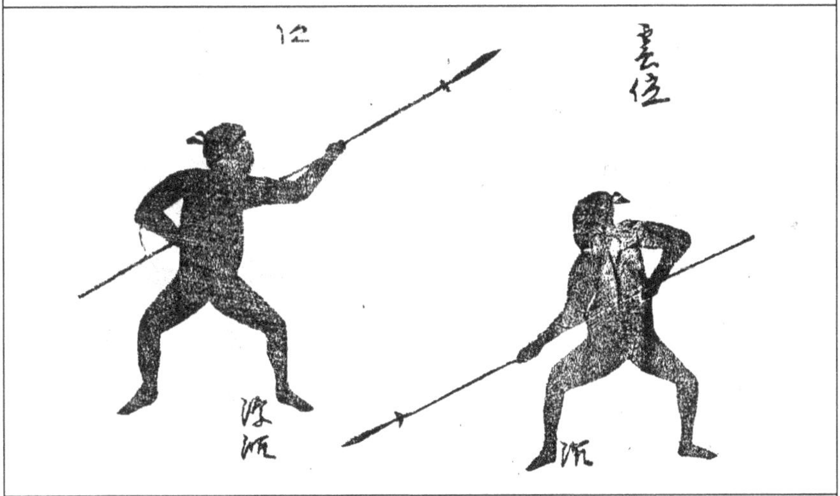

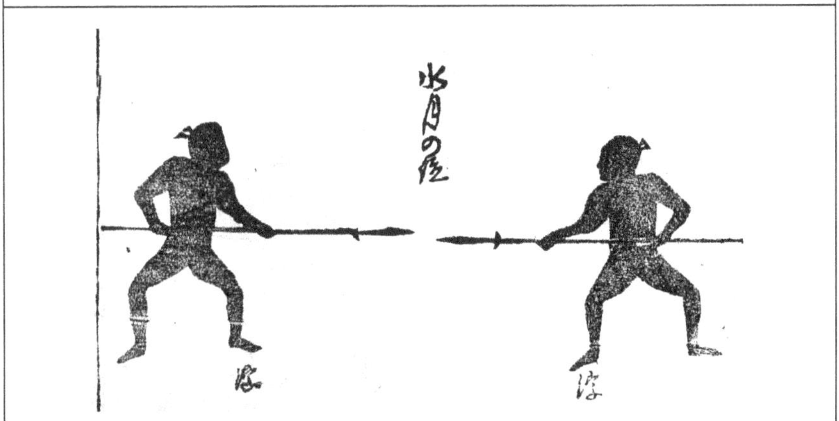

(Left and Right) 水月の位　浮 *Suigetsu no Kurai : Uki-Ashi*
Moon Reflected on Water Stance : Floating foot

中段
下段
電光位
下段電光の位

(Left)
下段電光の位沉 *Gedan : Denko no Kurai : Shizumu-Ashi*
Gedan : Lightning Bolt Stance : Planted foot

(Right)
中段清眼の位沉 *Chudan : Seigan no Kurai : Shizumu-Ashi*
Chudan : Clear-eyed Stance : Planted foot

(Left and Right)下段電光の位沉 Gedan : Denko no Kurai : Shizumu-Ashi
Gedan : Lightning Bolt Stance : Planted foot

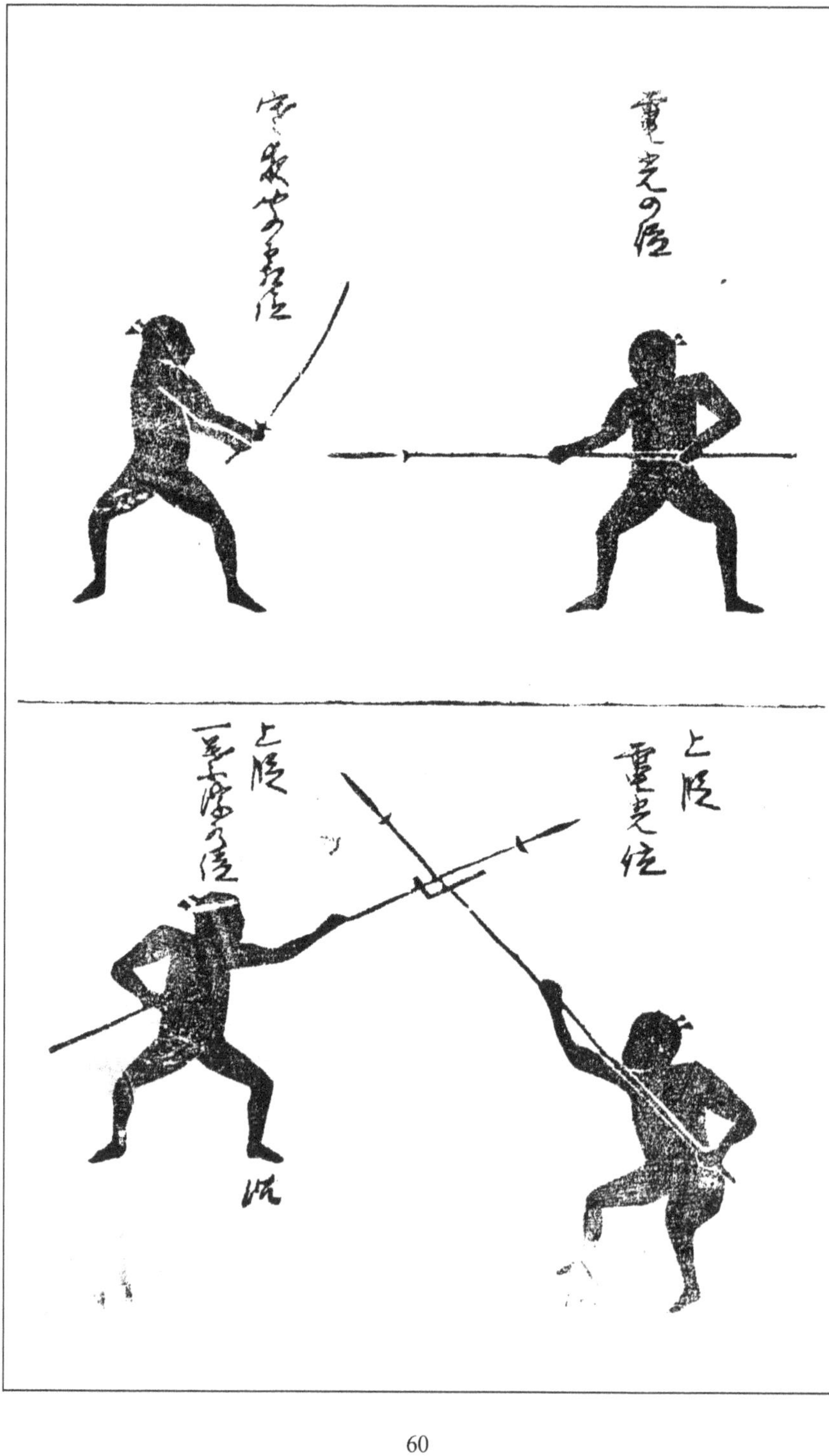

(Left)
上段寒夜聞霜の位 沈
*Kanyashimowokiku no Kurai Shizumu-Ashi*
Jodan : The stance of being able to hear frost crack on a winter's night : Planted foot
(Right) 上段電光の位沈 *Jodan: Denko no Kurai Shizumu-Ashi*
Jodan : Lightning Bolt Stance : Planted foot

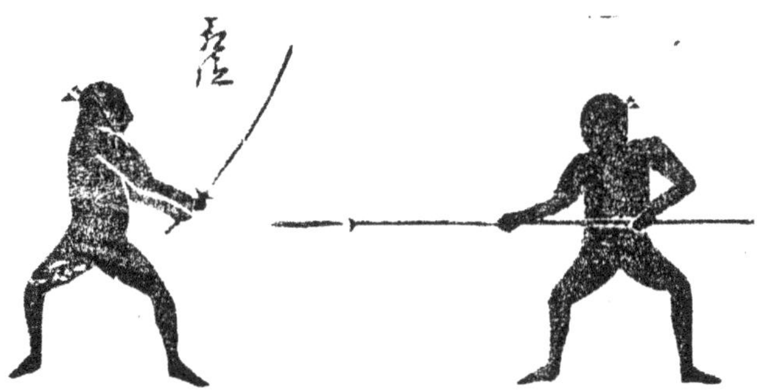

(Left)
上段 一葉浮水の位沉 Jodan *Ichiefusui no Kurai Shizumu-Ashi*
Jodan : Leaf floating upon water Stance : Planted Foot
(Right)
上段　電光の位沉 *Jodan Denko no Kurai : Shizumu-Ashi*
Jodan : Lightning Bolt Stance : Planted foot.

水月の位
中段
電光の位

水月の位　*Suigetsu no Kurai*
Moon Reflected on Water Stance

爰琴糸をきる　習ひあり 沉
Here there is a lesson about cutting the cord of the Koto (Koto is a kind of Japanese lute) Planted Foot
(Left)
中段電光の位浮　Chudan : Denko no Kurai : Uki-Ashi
Chudan : Lightning Bolt Stance : Floating foot

▲入身の事

世の人の身といふハ嘉力と名付て縫を主として十三字の経緯にて
まず身の本を元へたしかにして今嘉力わかるをもとにて又歌の
姿へをもする義なり門といふ是三ツの法なりあり歌花をさるやうに
そのは嘉力と後をあり上下のわたよりわが中後の姿を入てつくる事を
あるまふたるよりや正るまは遠近の法あるとも名付くのべし
是もあり歌を作る又これの事ふへあり

▲退け者仕様の事

退け者なる六二ツの事へ退退付の時ハ浮気のあひをも同く
下後をもよせ事しかるべきたちを見てもちかづきてまあるなら
又たちもくる時ハ退てを勢ひとねらふべし又ずして退のまゝを

## 入身の事

*Nyushin no Koto*

**Entering With Your Body**

Generally the meaning of the term Nyushin 入身 is to stop the movement of the Yari with the Tachi. You can also use a Juji-Kagi Yari, or a hooked cross shaped headed spear, to catch the opponent's spear and enter Temoto 手元, where the opponent's hands hold the spear. What is written here is a method for breaking the opponent's Kamae, or stance.

There are three ways of thinking for those entering the gate, which is another way of saying entering deep into the enemy's space. If you detect the Kehai 気配, or the intention, of the opponent you should take Daijodan no Kamae. Should you detect the enemy's Keihai coming from the right, you should go into Chudan Kamae while visualizing doing a Tsuki 突, or straight thrust. When you sense Keihai in front of you enter while staying aware the space near you and farther away as well. This is the best method for detecting the Keihai of the enemy.

## 追駆者仕留める事

*Oikake Mono no Shitomere Koto*

**How to Strike Down an Escaping Samurai**

With regards to pursuing a fleeing soldier there are two things taught. When striking while pursuing you should make use of techniques that have Uki-ashi and strike with a sweeping Gedan cut to the lower part of the body. You should take care with your distancing as though it seems you are close enough, you may end up missing your target entirely.

Should the enemy come about you should, initially, drop back a step thereby lessoning the opponent's energy. Here you are required to evaluate the relative distance near or far to the opponent. There is a Kuden.

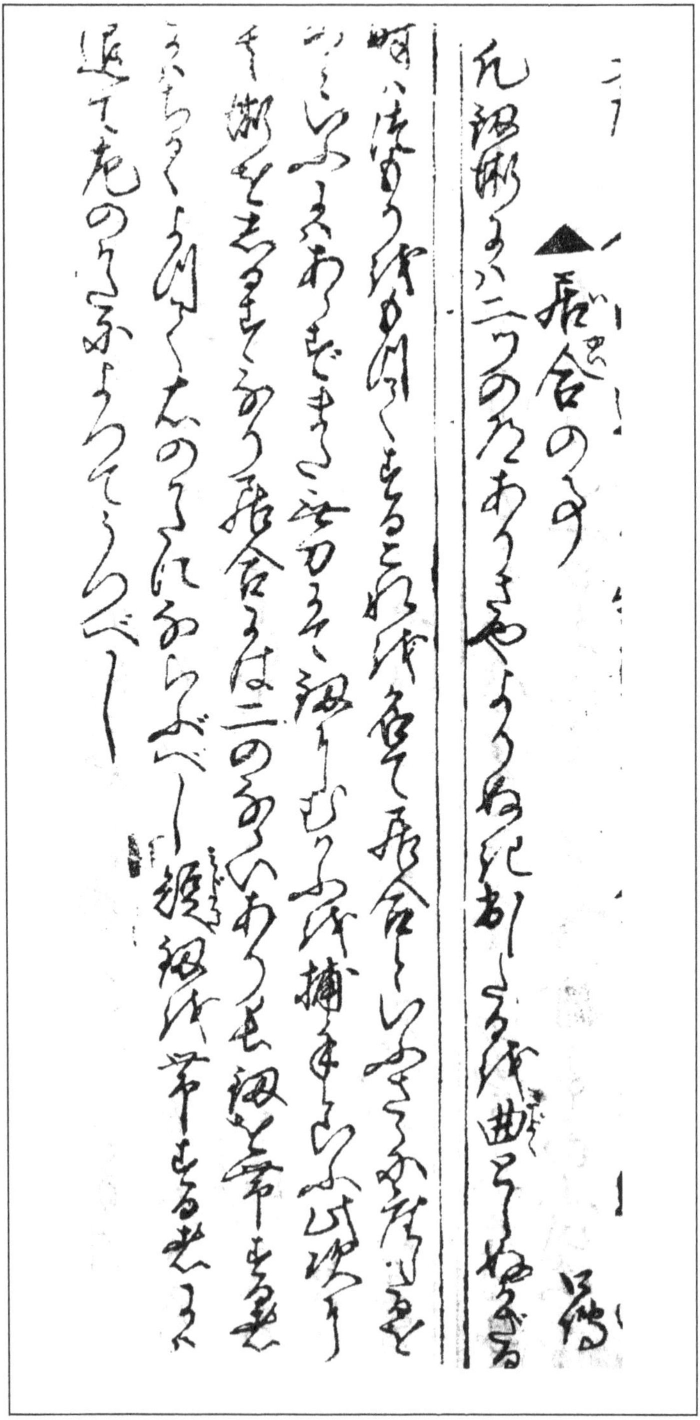

居合の事

## 居合の事
### *Iai no Koto*
### **Sword Drawing**

This section will have to be balanced with what was written in the previous chapters. This is the thing that has been given the name Iai. However, Iai is not done exclusively from a seated position. It can also refer to when you take down an opponent armed with a sword when you are Muto, or without a sword. Next that technique will be explained.

There are two techniques in Iai. For opponents with a long sword in their belt, close in until you are aligned with their right shoulder. For opponents with a short sword, you should drop back and cut in toward the opponent's right shoulder.

▲捕手のこと

捕手は兼て目に組討を學ざるものはちからより組をうご
つまを考ばいつらうてせんとる是三ツの要あるべし又よく
戦場にて組の勝負いまだして手足の働をみて戦を組
討といふ是よりその品れひとし紀分り給ふもひとつの心
得あり是を達と常するものはおそもいさまですすむる者なれ
おはいらむべしてるとの考をはるの事へ入り歩行あるべ
かつ組討捕手にて勝負ときるのとぶらつなせぬるなるべ

## 捕手(とりて)の事
### *Torite no Koto*
### **Unarmed Fighting**

Torite refers to when you are fighting without any sort of blade, long or short and you are against a person swinging a sword. You deceive this person and take the advantage with your Ashi Sabaki, or footwork, along with three main points. These will be briefly detailed below. Abbreviated below.

On the battlefield, when the swords do not end the fight, battling on with feet and hands is called Kumi Uchi. These are the same methods as the Torite Techniques. That being said there is a single way of thinking with regards to these. A person wearing Tabi will not injure his feet, a barefoot person will hurt his feet.

A mounted rider should be pulled from his horse while a foot soldier should be grabbed by the head and pulled down onto his back. A helmeted warrior should be pulled facedown. A shirtless many should be struck in the chest and the most important thing is to take the enemy's sword. Further, take great care that your own blade is not stolen away. This is a technique that holds or wraps up with the left hand while the right does the action.

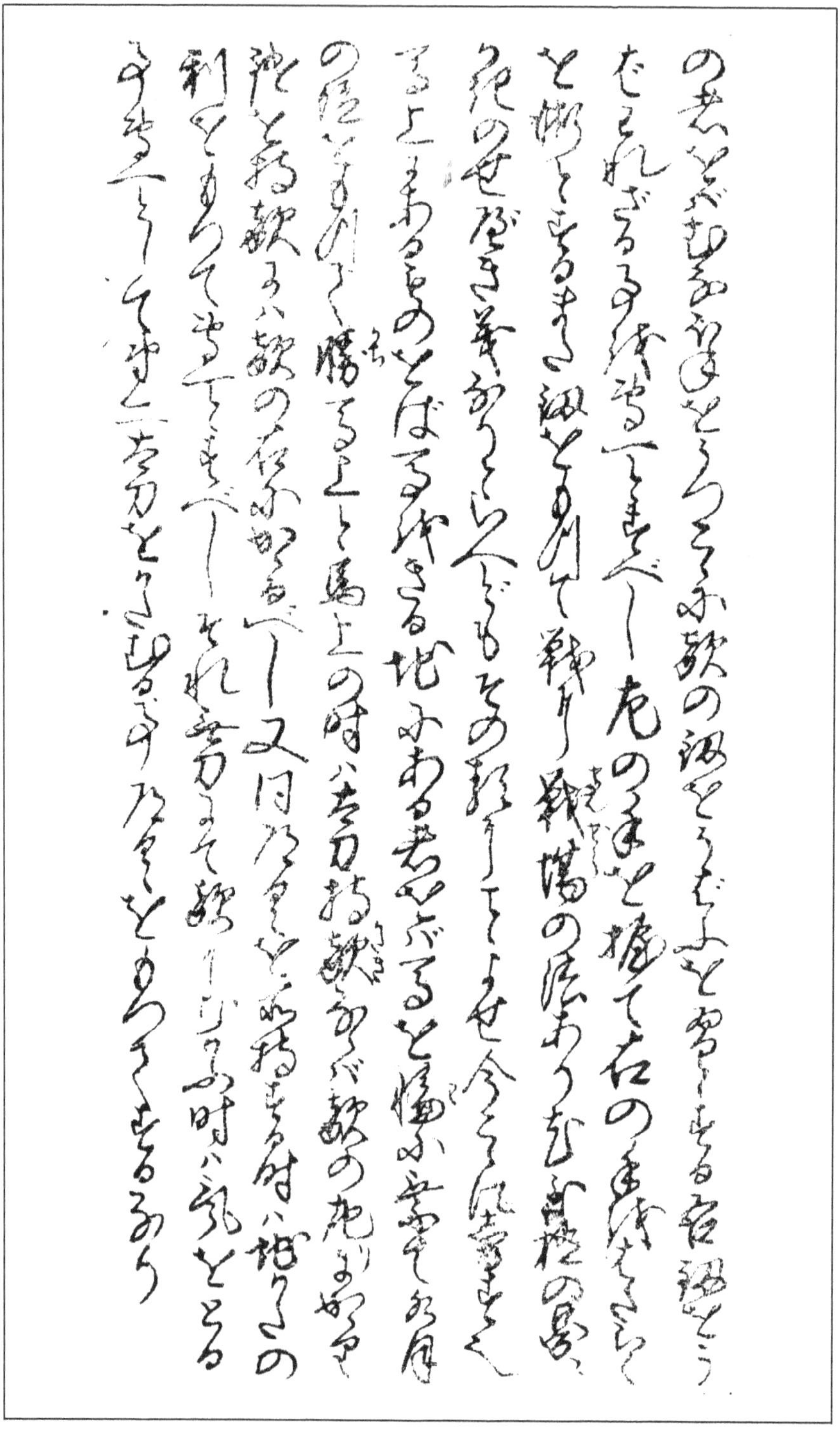

In addition, there is a way to fight whilst holding a sword. Typically an illustration of this extreme situation should be placed here in my opinion but as it is the same I will just write a description.

For a warrior on horseback, cut at the horse. For a man on the ground, trace a circle around him on your horseback and win with Suigetsu no Kurai.

For situations where both are mounted on horseback. If the opponent is holding a Tachi, attack from the opponents left. An opponent holding a spear should be met on the right. These attacking methods are essential.

Further, in the case where you are both armed with the same weapon, it is important to make use of Chi no Ri, or the advantage of the terrain, to your best advantage. In addition, when Muto, or without a sword, and facing off against an enemy the most important thing is Kisen wo Sei Suru 機先を制する, or take the advantage by striking first in an unexpected manner. From there you should next completely block the movement of the enemy's sword and take his weapon away from him.

▲がんせきくわせきのこと

はなはだ[illegible]百[illegible]め地にして上を度々て[illegible]難く

[illegible]と積る年もまた二三百年の間[illegible]にみゆる

おつる[illegible]などは時々[illegible]なおして別たちあり

## がんせきくだきの事
### *Gansekikudaki no Koto*
### Crushing a Great Rock

The weighted portion of this is formed from a hundred Monme 匁, or 375 grams, of lead. Form it into a ball and cover it with skin. Sew up the seam where the two ends of the hide overlap and attach a short cord. An opponent can be struck between the eyebrows from between two and three Ken, or 3.6 to 5.4 meters/yards away. In the summer or other warmer times striking the chest bone will immediately cause a man to crumple.

| | |
|---|---|
|  | この土は袂(たもと)に入れて持ち運ぶ事<br>You should place this ball in your Tamoto 袂, or sleeve, and carry it about with you. |

(Written inside the circle) You should place this ball in your Tamoto 袂, or sleeve, and carry it about with you.
The Sakurai scroll contains the following:
You absolutely cannot use this technique without the express permission of your lord.
This document is a military strategy scroll based on what was revealed by Kusunoki Masashige. It is a secret military document. For further information please refer to the Heihoki.

In the end, the learning of Kenjutsu and Jujutsu are by order of the lord. All of the rest of your studies should be concerned with guarding your principals. Of essence is that you maintain both discretion and a straightforward mindset.
Rather than learning Kenjutsu and then proceeding to travel down a mountain road frequented by bandits you should not take up the study of Kenjutsu and stay afraid of such roads. Thus you will stay safe. You should not forget that there is a Kotowaza 諺, or saying that goes, Nama Byoho wa Okega no Moto 生兵法は大怪我の元. A little bit of military learning will only result in big injuries.

▲早縄の事

早縄と云ハ人を捕へて早く縄をかけ申事也白縄

或ハ方によりからかけかゝる所乃縄を多くおさえ

縄の如くもす又人中を捕て縄とつる又ハ寄も替る也

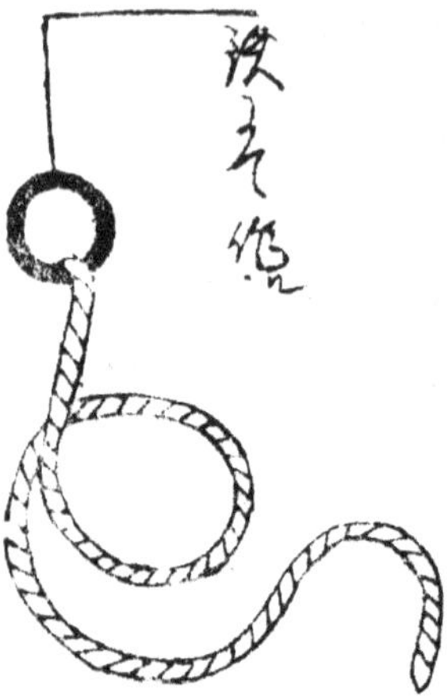


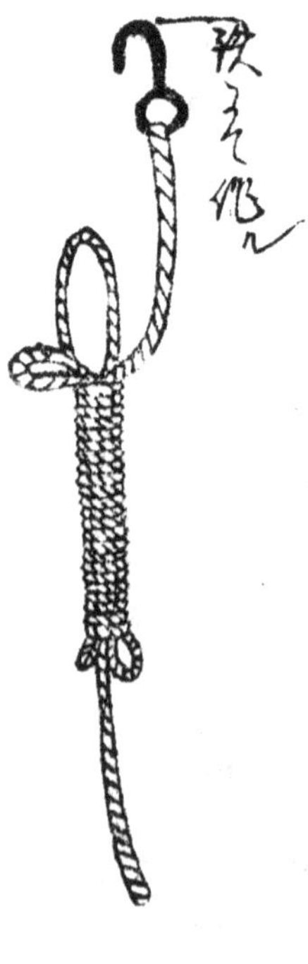


右九ヶ条口傳あり

## 早縄の事
## *Hayanawa no Koto*
## **Fast Tie Binding**

Hayanawa refers to a method for quickly restraining a person by rapidly tying them up with rope. Typically a long thick rope of Five Shaku, or 1.5 meters is used. On the end of that a hook is attached. A ring is also sometimes used.

There is a Kuden related bringing the rope in to the right.

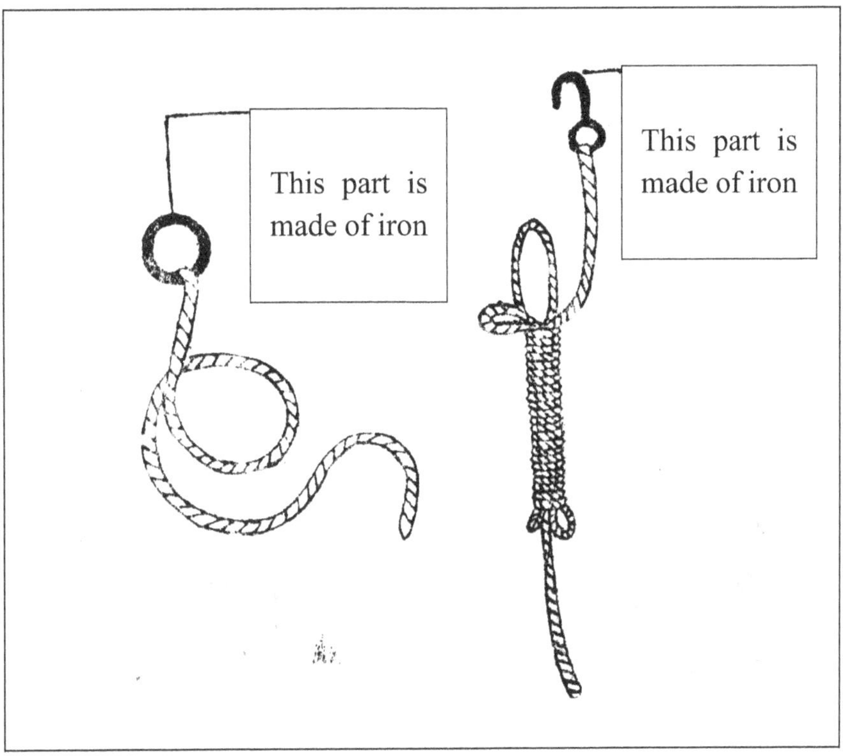

△元結共ニ所ある事

元結共おゝくば出来を賤しとすべし侍ハ時服をくれて諸くなる
下部ハ時服をくれて諸くなる也なり

△鍼術虚実の事

凡鍼術の虚実といふハ上脘を討んと見せて下脘をうち下脘
と見せて中脘とするなり所をしりて当るとうちまへ至る事あり
急ニ来る敵ハひらいて討べし出るやうに来る敵ハ中脘のまへ
可しるべし退敵の勝負を見るの肝要なり

△薬術あての事

凡薬術といふハ敵の手足を遮るべし又あて所ハ其
のあてとて鍼術あて又ひきて本脈のあたりて下もハ陰の経
おのれハ引しときとるべし

## 取籠者に心得すること
### *Torikomori Mono ni Kokoroe suru Koto*
### **How to Handle a Samurai You Have Surrounded**

If you have surrounded a person, the first thing you should do in find out who they are. If the person is a Bushi, or Samurai, they will become stronger as time passes. If it is a person of lower status however they will become weaker as time passes.

## 剣術虚実(きょじつ)の事
### *Kenjutsu Kyojitsu no Koto*
### **Using Truth and Falsehood With the Sword**

For the most part within Kenjutsu, the sword arts, the term Kyo-Jitsu, or Truth-Falsehood refer to showing that you are going to cut in from Jodan when you actually are going to cut from Gedan. Show that you are going to cut from Gedan and then cut in from Chudan. It is of the upmost importance to keep this concept in mind as you go into Kamae with the Tachi.

For an opponent that enters quickly, you should open up to one side and strike. For an opponent that attacks slowly it is best to go into Chudan. That being said it is important to watch the opponent's eyes.

A person whose eyes are red (signifying a person who is wound up) should be handled calmly. However a person whose eyes are white (a brave warrior) should be dealt with using sudden violent attacks.

## 柔術、当身(あてみ)の事
### *Jujutsu Atemi no Koto*
### **On the Subject of Jujutsu and Atemi, or Striking**

For the most part Jujutsu refers to using a joint lock on the opponent's feet or legs. Further, Atemi striking refers to striking the chest or the area under the armpits. Also striking between the eyes. Below that are points like Kage no Fu, the solar plexus, which if struck is something that cannot be endured.

▲夜の太刀秘伝の事

夜中に我寝所にしのび入の者あらば二刀上段のかまへを

ありてもよし 寝所のうちやうをよくよくさぐりかくし 敵のきたるをうかがひ

まちうけ候ふべし 又太刀のさばきにおいてはとうけてさぐる事

あり是ハ太刀をみじかくもつこころへなり

## 夜の太刀、秘術の事
### *Yoru no Tachi Hijutsu no Koto*
### The Secret Technique of Sword Fighting at Night

If you are in your bedroom in the middle of the night and you detect something suspicious, then you should go into Daijodan with your Tachi. Turn the Saya, or scabbard, so it is straight up and down, which will protect you from a waist level cut from the opponent. Further, you can also place the Saya on the end of the sword. You should keep in mind that the feet should be used to maximize the length of the Tachi.

▲眼つけの事

武家におゐて官位ある身をまもりて天下泰平の時を
へて世におゐて後をまもりて今におゐて敵なき守護が
有つる文武も、ともに修行して兵法の武芸をうけて、その家に伝はる
学びを立て構へて第一の所において敵にむかはず
徳へ入りて此流を学ぶ人見るべし 初心の修行は夜昼ともに
是は山中動静がありて兵法の稽古ありて候 兵
法は見るべし 軍見智術兵術も君命のかは執事を
そのかれが今生を主として修行すべし智術
を知て鑑識の書を山林を通りて入かは智術をもつて
人が心してまなぶるが勝負とするべし読して兵法大意
の基となるべく候まで

## 眼潰しの事
### *Metsubushi no Koto*
### **On the Topic of Metsubushi, Blinding powders**

Open a small hole in an egg's shell. Blow out the contents and fill it with powdered Togarashi, or red pepper, and cover the hole with paper. Then put it in your Tamoto, or end of the sleeve of your Kimono. When you are faced with an enemy smash it on their face. Also you can bury a poisonous Mamushi snake in the ground and pile horse manure on top. Add finely chopped grass and mix it. After powdering it, roll it in paper tissue like you would use to wipe your nose. Blowing it at an opponent will cause them to lose consciousness. This method is rather incomplete and has not been fully tested. You should probably rely more on the teachings of your master and not attempt it without his permission. This is but an extract of the Record of Military Strategy left to us by Yamamoto Kansuke.

In the end it is essential to understand that both Kenjutsu and Jujutsu are not only to protect the life of your lord but are tools with which you can protect yourself and keep yourself on the correct path. Despite knowing Kenjutsu it is best to err on the side of caution and not enter a mountain road infested with brigands. There is a saying that goes "A little bit of military training can be the cause of great injury."

# 軍法兵法記　奥義巻

▲敵二人我一人仕合之事

夫敵ハ二人我ハ一人にて仕合ときハ二人のてきを向ふにうけて右の方れ敵よかゝる氣色をよこうせて左の敵へ出廻るべし右の方れ敵後へ廻らんとせバわきへひらきて左の方の敵を撃べし

# 軍法兵法記・奥義の巻

# Military Strategy and Sword Fighting *Ogi no Maki* - The Inner Secrets Scroll

### 敵二人、我一人試合の事
### *Teki Futari, Ware Hitori Shiai no Koto*
### When You Are Alone Against Two Attackers

The learning of Kenjutsu and Jujutsu are by the order of the lord however all other study should be devoted to keeping yourself on the true path and preserving your integrity. This is very important. When you are alone and facing two opponents, position yourself so you are standing opposite both of them. Give the impression that you are going to attack the opponent on your right, then join combat with the enemy on your left.

Note: This is a separate book contained within Way of the Sword.

一 敵(てき)一人味方(みかた)多勢(たぜい)仕合の事

夫敵一人にて味方二人ならバ前後(せんご)よりうつべし二人の時ハ三方よりうつべし四人のときハ四方よりうつべし多勢各此理を知るべし

## 敵一人、味方多数試合の事

### *Teki Hitori, Mikata Tasu Shiai no Koto*

### Fighting Against One Person With Many Soldiers

If there is but a single enemy soldier and two of your warriors, one of you should attack from behind. If there are three of you then strike in from three different directions. If there are four of you attack from four different directions. For greater numbers follow this same principal.

▲川中仕合之事

夫川中まて歩立の仕合ハ敵を川上よりおとされへてきの方下をさしのひよ立向べし其理ハ身一ツにおもてむかふハ陽性をうくる理身二ツ川上より流れ来る物の難をうけざる理あるを以なり

▲又のてち十あい

## 川中試合の事
### *Kawanaka Shiai no Koto*
### Fighting in the Middle of a River

When fighting a battle in a river you should position your forces so that the enemy is upstream from you. You should be on the right-hand side, diagonally opposite the enemy. The underlying theory here is, first of all, if you are facing the flow of the river you can receive the Yosei 陽性, or combined energy of the opponent and the river. Second, scraps of wood and so forth that flow down from upstream will not cause a damage to your forces.

If during the afternoon the sunlight should be to your back. If you are armed with Yari 鑓, or spears, then your forces should be placed at the Mizu-giwa 水際, or where the water meets the land. They should strike from Gedan Kamae. This will help to conserve your energy.

▲家内仕合の事

夫家内にて仕合すんハ先天井の高さをしるべし鴨居と敷居とに工夫して是ハ勝手に居て敵をなやんずる所にかまへべし又其の者が家内にしてハ時刻をのばすべし他の家内にして即時に勝をとるべし

▲日中仕合の事

夫日中に仕合ときハ日を背に受べし気栄りしなる利有又敵を日に向はすれバ目まふくして我が色めをとらぬものなり

▲月夜仕合の事

夫月夜に仕合ときハ我ハ陰の方に居て敵を月に向はすべしそのまゝかくれて敵をあやつりたるの利なり

## 家内(かない)試合の事
***Kanai Shiai no Koto***
**Fighting in a House**

Should you ever have to join combat within a house you should first gauge the height of the ceiling as well as the distance to the walls on your right and left. Next, you should consider your Joyo 助用 or the spot which is the most advantageous for you, in addition to your Nansho 難所, or your weak point in the room. Devise a Kufu, or device, that will allow you to be set up in the beneficial Joyo position. At the same time the enemy should be forced into the most difficult position, the Nansho.

Further, if you are within your own home try to delay the confrontation as much as possible. Should you be in a dwelling not your own then try to end the confrontation as quickly as possible.

## 日中(にっちゅう)試合の事
***Nicchu Shiai no Koto***
**Fighting During Midday**

When fighting during the day be sure to have the sun at your back. You will receive a beneficial push of Ki 気 or spirit. Further, the sun will be bright in the enemy's eyes and they will not be able to read the faces of your men.

## 月夜(つきよ)試合の事
***Tukiyo Shiai no Koto***
**Fighting on a Moonlit Night**

When fighting at night under a moon lit sky, you should place your forces in the shadow and the moonlight in the enemy's face. The benefit is that you will be hidden and the faces of the enemy will be clearly illuminated.

▲闇夜仕合之事

夫やみのよの仕合といふハ弓を志川にて敵のうちを
とりえをうし[illegible]れいるをとるべし前難およあ
らば我まへ小敵て仕合なさすり

▲敵我後ニ来披事

夫敵我後よりきたりて云をうけうしんとする白
とききハ右の方にむくきて利あるなり

## 闇夜(やみよ)試合の事

*Yamiyo Shiai no Koto*

**Fighting on a Dark Night**

When battling on a dark night drop your body down low and concentrate on the formation the enemy has taken and try to determine how they are armed. Note however that should the terrain not be to your advantage you should move in and engage the enemy. It can be beneficial to conceal your forces in a dark place in order to spy on the enemy.

## 敵が後方から来た時、披(ひら)く事

*Teki ga Koho Kara Kita Toki, Hiraku Koto*

**Opening up When Attacked From Behind**

If an enemy approaches from behind and calls out to you as he cuts in, the best defense is to move out to the right. This will all be to the enemy's disadvantage.

◢敵顔色形持やうの事

夫斬合仕合の時ニ当て敵の顔色を見るニおゐて

なるへく性気上るいろ色あり性気のさかる則は

勝利工夫ある事もおゝくいせるしくあるものなり

次ハ顔色悪く白なるハ心虚なる謂なり心おくある●

しきニハ命をおしむものなり命をおしむ則ハ向をうけ

居さ勝利をうしなふへし進んすとのそむ手ありの

やうり敵の顔持を見て利をとる事ハ敵を

みると思ふをとさせてるしあり下をみるときハ

近きをみると云ふ處あり

## 敵顔色顔持見る事
### *Teki Kao Iro Kao Mochi Miru Koto*
### **Observing the Enemy's Face**

It is important to look at the face of your enemy when you are set to engage in a Kiri-Ai 斬り合い or a sword fight. If the face has become red then the enemy is not in their right mind. As they have become unstrung it is not necessary to resort to a Kufu. Their spirit is not settled.

Next, if the face is pale it is evidence of a person who is fearful. When a person is fearful they value their life greatly and are unlikely to strike first. Such a person is not thinking about winning, only of escaping.

Further, in order to gain an advantage by judging the enemy's face, know that when the opponent is looking up he is observing something in the distance. When looking downward he is observing something nearby. It is important not to Yudan 油断, or become careless or miscalculate here.

▲足場悪地にて仕合する事

夫足場悪き地にて仕合には身をかるがるとしての利を
ちからとすべし若又前は足場あしくして後へあしべ[illegible]
あらば我先足場あしき地に居て時を移て敵は足場
能地に退欲をあしぞあしき地に動べし

## <ruby>足場悪地<rt>あしばあくち</rt></ruby>にて試合の事

***Ashiba Akuchi Ni Te Shiai no Koto***

**Fighting on Uneven Ground**

Should you have to engage in combat in a place where the footing is poor, first of all it is best not to move your body around. You should also consider how you can use the situation to your advantage. For example, if the footing is bad on the ground in front of you and behind you it is good, place yourself in the area of bad footing. When the enemy makes their way over to you move to the more solid ground thereby placing the enemy forces on bad footing.

# Way of the Sword

# End

### Additional Material

# Researching Yamamoto Kansuke

Illustration from *Yamamoto Kansuke* by Shiba Nanso. 1920

I had to go through a great deal of material in order to complete this translation and found many interesting details. This next section introduces snippets from some of the sources I consulted to complete this translation.

In the early Edo Period, the era following the Warring States Period, the only reference to Yamamoto Kansuke was in the Koyo Gunkan. The book states that he was born in the second year of Meiou (1493) and was killed on September eighteenth of the fourth year of Eiroku (1561) during the fourth Kawanakajima Battle. There are additional accounts of his birth having taken place in the 9th year of Meiou (1500) as well as in the first year of Bunki (1501). His Inami, or royal name, was Haruyuki and after he left his former domain his name became Tohki. The Koyo Gunkan describes Kansuke as a military strategist and builder of castles. Virtually no other document relating to him existed.

During the ninth year of Genroku (1696) Matsuura Shigenobu published his work called A Record of Various and Sundry Military Successes. In his work he concluded that it was Yamamoto Kansuke's son who crafted the mythos surrounding Yamamoto Kansuke. It was this son that wrote the Koyo Gunkan and falsely attributed the document to Kosaka Danjo (Kasuka Masanobu). Matsuura's overall conclusion did not deny that Yamamoto Kansuke existed but rather dismissed notion that he was a military strategist and right-hand man to Takeda Shingen and relegated him to the status of a low-level retainer of Yamagata Clan.

The Meiji Era saw the release of Tokyo University professor Tanaka Yoshinari's Considerations Regarding the Koyo Gunkan in 1891. Professor Tanaka concluded that as a historical document the Koyo Gunkan should not be considered reliable. Further, as the Koyo Gunkan was an entirely fabricated document likely written entirely by Obata Kagenori, (1572–1663) a Confucian scholar and retainer of the Takeda, both it and Yamamoto Kansuke were not appropriate materials for serious research.

In the 34$^{th}$ year of the Showa Era (1959) Okuno Takahiro wrote the book Takeda Shingen. In it he wrote that Yamamoto Kansuke was in fact an entirely fictional character. The reason for this being that Takeda Shingen would never have given the kanji 晴 Haru to Kansuke as he himself received it from the Muromachi Shogun.

However, ten years later in 1969, the short period drama about Takeda Shingen called Heaven and Earth aired on NHK television. A certain Mr. Ichikawa of Hokkaido happened to see the show and recognized the Kao, or signature of Takeda Shingen as being on some documents that had been handed down in his family. They were authenticated at Hokkaido University. One of the documents, written in 1557 was from Takeda Shingen to a lord Ichikawa Fujiwaka. Taneda wroth the letter in thanks for Ichikawa's efforts in causing the forces of Uesugi Kenshin to withdraw. At the end of the letter it indicated that the bearer of the message, Yamamoto Kansuke, had other details to relay. The revelation confirmed not only that Yamamoto Kansuke existed but that he occupied a position of some status, opening up the possibility that he was a military strategist with whom Takeda Shingen consulted and not a low-level retainer.

**Excerpt from:**
**武功雑記 *Buko Zakki***
**Assorted Tales of Martial Bravery**
**by Matsuura Shigenobu 松浦鎮信 著**

Yamamoto Kansuke by 歌川豊国 Utagawa Toyokuni (1802-1835)

There was a man by the name of Kami Izumi Nobutsuna Ise no Kami (1508?-1572?) who was a master of Heiho, or the art of the sword. He, along with his disciple named Kohaku (Hikita Kagetoma 1537?-1605?) made their way to Senshu, modern day Osaka.

At the time, Yagyu Muneyoshi was the unparalleled master of Kenjutsu in this region. Upon hearing of Kami Izumi's visit, he was trilled and called upon him to show some techniques with the Bokken wooden practice sword. Upon seeing the demonstration, he was captivated and requested a duel.

"If you must, but first I think you should face Kohaku first." Said Kami Izumi.

Muneyoshi pressed his case but Kami Izumi rebuffed him thrice. In the end Yagyu Muneyoshi stood before Kohaku.

"Your form looks bad all around." said Kohaku. And with that, he struck Muneyoshi a total of three times. However, Muneyoshi repeated his request.

"I humbly request a bout with Lord Kami Izumi!" As it would have been difficult for Kami Izumi to decline again he stood before Muneyoshi.

"Well then, well then...I suppose I will just have to take that Tachi from you."

With that, Kami Izumi moved in and plucked the Tachi out of Muneyoshi's hands. Muneyoshi was thunderstruck. Kami Izumi remained there for three years and in that interval passed on the teachings that became Yagyu Shinkage Ryu.

Later, requesting a leave of absence Kami Izumi moved onto the Kanto region of eastern Japan. He ended up in Mikawa no Kuni Ushikubo, modern day Aichi Prefecture. In Ushikubo a man by the name of Makinoshi oversaw a fiefdom worth three thousand Koku. One of his retainers, Yamamoto Kansuke was a practitioner of Kyo Ryu Kenjutsu (which was written as either 京流 or 行流). Kansuke was quite proud and made several snide remarks about the arrival of Kami Izumi and his disciple.

"If they want to meet, I, Kansuke, will give them a thrashing." Kansuke said this and other things. Lord Makinoshi summoned both Kansuke and Kami Izumi and told them he desired to see a bout between them.

"Very well, but why don't we have Kohaku go first." Said Kami Izumi. Kohaku immediately stood before Kansuke and said, "Your form looks bad all around." With that he struck Kansuke without any apparent difficulty. Returning to the starting positions they began again.

Next Kohoku declared, "I believe I will take that from you." And he moved in and took the Tachi out of Kansuke's hands. Everyone that saw the bout was stunned. Amongst the spectators there were those that were decidedly against Kansuke and they jeered, "Kansuke you were struck bad!"

Angered and humiliated Kansuke asked for a leave of absence from Makinoshi and made his way to Kai no Kuni. Kai no Kuni was welcoming to Samurai from other regions and they were particularly delighted to have someone from Mikawa. "Kansuke is adept at the sword but is a man of few words (this same phrase has also been interpreted as he was an eloquent speaker).

No one there had heard of Kansuke. Later, during one of the Kawanakajima battles, Yamagata Masakage sent Kansuke out on a reconnaissance mission. Returning from his mission, Yamamoto Kansuke went to report to Yamagata. Upon seeing him Takeda Shingen said, "Who is that man?"
"That is Yamamoto Kansuke, he is from Mikawa. He receives a stipend from Yamagata and is under his command." However, other than this there was nothing remarkable about Yamamoto Kansuke.

Kansuke's son was a monk of the Kanzan Order at Myoshinji Temple who had some proficiency with his letters. While in Koshu no Kuni, modern day Yamanashi Prefecture, he gathered many scraps and snippets of information regarding Takeda Shingen and liberally added or attributed some of the information to his father Yamamoto Kansuke. Having made the book he then falsely attributed it to Kosaka Danjo (Kosaka Masanobu 1527-1578).

Later, gathering information from a member of the Li Naotaka household who was from Koshu , he gathered more information about Koshu. He called this work the Koyo Gunkan. This book is of course entirely a work of fiction.

## Translation of Historic Letters Regarding Yamamoto Kansuke

In recent years several sets of important Sengoku Era (16th century) documents have come to light. In 1969 a family watching a television drama about the 16th century general Takeda Shingen. The producers of the show had been meticulous with the recreation which included accurately reproducing documents and letters exchanged on the show. The family noticed in these scenes the official seals resembled the seals on a set of old documents that had been handed down in the family for generations. These were eventually authenticated and became known as the *Ichikawa Documents*. Later the Mashimo Family documents and others were discovered and many details of Kansuke's life were confirmed.

This next section presents translations of some of the important documents, beginning with the *Letter to Lord Ichikawa*, which was the first mention of Yamamoto Kansuke during the Sengoku Era.

**Letter From Takeda Shingen to Ichikawa Fujiwaka. 1558.**

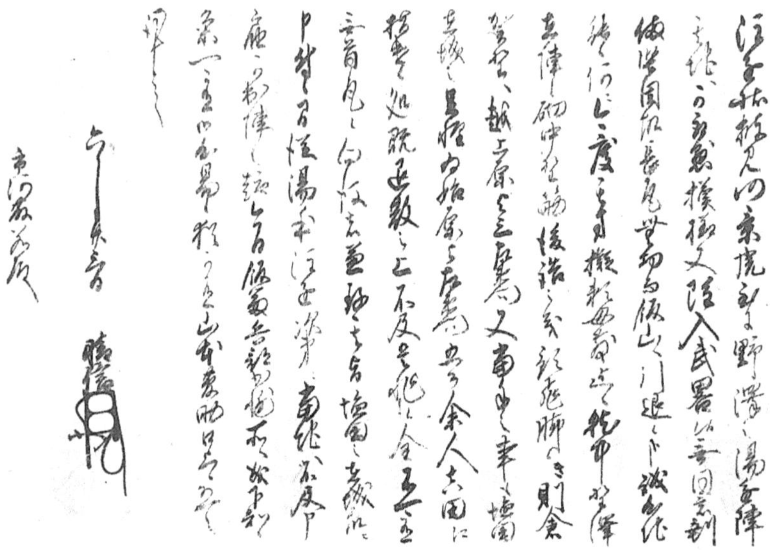

注進状披見仍景虎至于野沢湯進陣
其地へ可取懸模様又雖入武略候無同意剰
備堅固故長尾無功而飯山へ引退候哉誠心地
能候何ニ今度其方擬頼母敷迄候就中野沢
在陣候砌中野筋後詰之義預飛脚候き則倉
賀野へ越上原与三左衛門尉又当手之事も塩田
在城之足軽為始原与左衛門尉五百余人真田江
指遣候処既退散之上不及是非候全不可有
無首尾候向後者兼存其旨塩田之在城衆ニ
申付候間従湯本注進次第ニ当地へ不及申
届可出陣之赴今日飯富兵部少輔所へ成下知候
条可有御心易候猶可有山本菅助口上候恐々
謹言

六月廿三日　晴信（花押）

市河藤若殿

I have read your report regarding your movements. Kagetora (Uesugi Kenshin) is, at present, moving his forces toward the Nozawa Hot Springs and it appears he is planning to advance on your position. I had my vanguard assault him however his defenses were strong and we did not break through. However, the fact that Uesugi had to withdraw to Iiyama mountain without any success is truly a splendid outcome.

While Nagao Kagetora (Uesugi Kenshin) was in Nozawa I sent troops on a fast march to try and block his retreat to Nakano. I ordered Hara Yosan Saemon, who was in Kuragano to assist in this and he gathered five hundred Ashigaru troops that were in Shioda Castle. Moving under the command of Sanada Yukio, Yosan Saemon and his troops moved to block the withdrawal but it turns out they were not in time to prevent Uesugi from moving out of the area. Just to be clear, this is not a case of someone being at fault.

I am planning to leave instructions with those stationed at Shioda Castle. Please send any report you may have there. I have told Obu Hyobuno Sho that he does not need to wait for my approval but to set out with his forces as soon as he sees fit. You can rest assured that reinforcements are on the way.

Yamamoto Kansuke has some other details to relay.

Very Truly Yours

Third Year of Koji (1558) June 23rd Harunobu (Takeda Shingen) Kao (Signature)

To Lord Ichikawa Fujiwaka

Translator's Note: This letter is so awesome. No evidence of Yamamoto Kansuke outside of the Koyo Gunkan for hundreds of years and suddenly *Bam!* "..any questions? Ask the guy handing you this missive, Yamamoto Kansuke."

**A Letter From Takeda Shingen to Yamamoto Kansuke. 1548.**

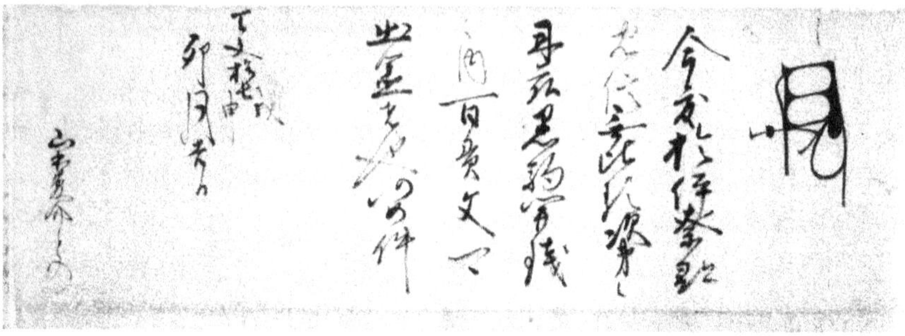

（晴信花押）
今度於伊奈郡
忠信無比類次第候
因茲黒駒関銭
之内百貫文可
出置者也仍如件
天文拾七　戊申
卯月吉日

Harunobu's (Takeda Shingen's) Kao Signature

The other day you did a bang-up job in Inaguma (Present day Nagano Prefecture). As I owe you a great debt of gratitude I hope you will accept a hundred Kan (approximately 200 Koku/ money for enough rice for 200 people for one year) from the treasury at Kurogoma. I have passed on the order for this to happen.
Seventeenth Year of Tenbun (1548) Boshin (45th of the Sexagenary Cycle)
An Auspicious Day in March
To Lord Yamamoto Kansuke

**From Takeda Shingen to Yamamoto Kansuke. 1549.**

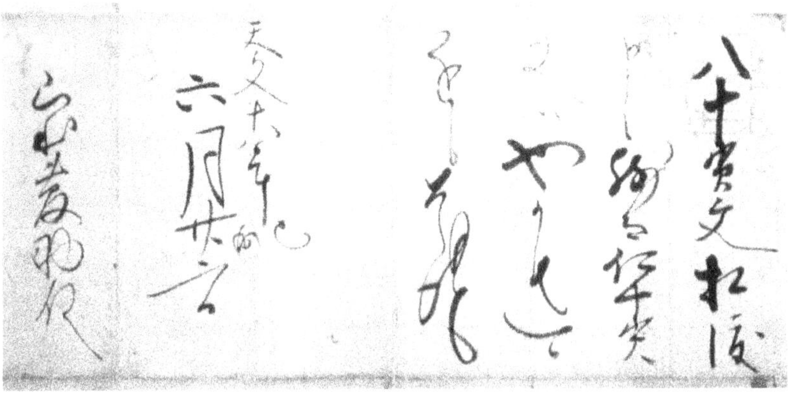

八十貫文相渡
申候、残而仁十貫
文ハ、やかて可
進候、恐々謹言、
天文十八年西乙
六月廿二日
山本勘助殿

(Stamp Unclear on Document)
A payment of eighty Kan is given.
The remaining twenty Kan will be paid at a later date.
Going forward with great respect

Eighteenth Year of Tenbun (1549)
June Twenty second
To Lord Yamamoto Kansuke

The letters regarding Kansuke continue on into the next generation. Here is a letter to the second-generation Yamamoto Kansuke who was 16 at the time. He was later killed in the Battle of Nagashino in 1575, at the age of 23. His successor was Yamamoto Jusaemon, a brother adopted before his birth.

**Letter from Takeda Shingen to Yamamoto Kansuke. 1568.**

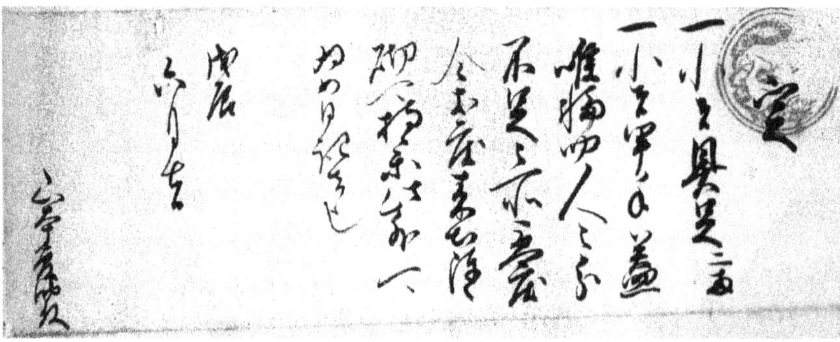

（龍朱印）定
一、小物具足二両
一、小物甲手蓋
喉輪四人之分
不足之所急渡
令支度来出陣之
砌可持参此外可
為如日記物也
戊辰　六月七日
山本菅助殿

Dragon Stamp (of Takeda Shingen)
One: Two sets of armor for low Level Komono soldiers
One: Gloves and Arm Coverings for Low level Komono Soldiers
Neck ring armor for four people. Anything else that may be lacking and you can pass on. As soon as you are ready, you should depart. You can carry things other than on this list. Be sure to have writing implements
Narishin June Seventeenth
To Lord Yamamoto Kansuke

## Letter from Takeda Shingen to Yamamoto Jusaemon. 1576.

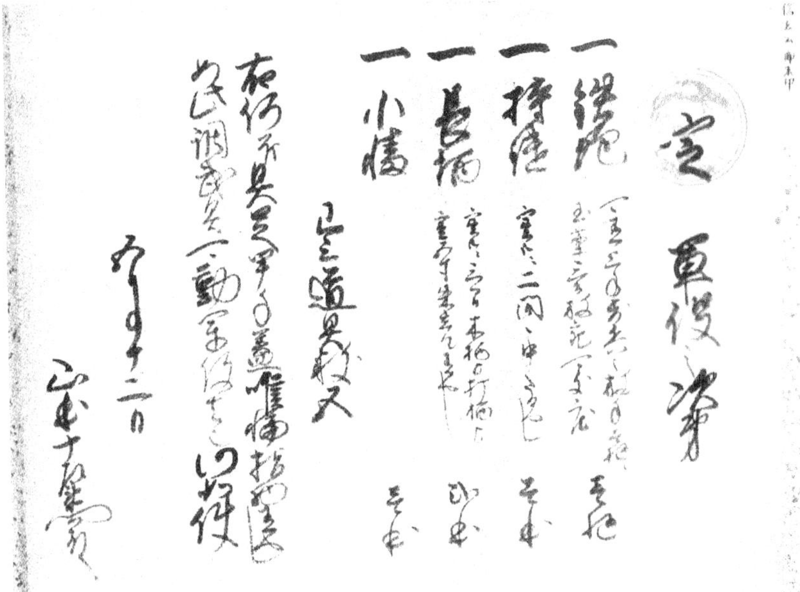

| | | |
|---|---|---|
| （龍朱印）定　軍役之次第 | | |
| 一、鉄砲 | 可有上手歩兵之放手一挺<br>玉薬三百放宛可支度 | 壱挺 |
| 一、持鎚 | 実共二二間之中たるへし | 壱本 |
| 一、長柄 | 実共二三間木柄歟打柄歟<br>実五寸朱志て有へし | 弐本 |
| 一、小幡 | | 壱本 |

巳上道具数五

右何茂具足・甲・手蓋・喉輪・指者有へし

如此調武具可勤軍役者也仍如件

五月十二日

山本十左衛門尉殿

Dragon Seal   Official    Orders are as follows

**Muskets:** Equip a foot soldier who is good with a rifle one rifle as well as prepare ball and powder for three hundred shots. One gun.
**Hand Spear:** Should be about two Ken in length (12 Shaku/ 12 feet) One spear.
**Long Shafted Weapons (Spear):** Both should be a length of 3 Ken (18 Shaku-18feet)with wooden handles or Uchi-e style wire wrapped bamboo handles. The blade should be about five Sun (15cm/ 6 inches)
**Small flag:** One Flag

That is all. Total number of items is five.
In addition to the items listed to the right you should have armor, a helmet, grieves, a throat plate and Sashimono identifying flags. Having prepared all of these items, report as such to your commander.
May Twelfth    (Tensei 4/1576)
To Lord Yamamoto Jusaemon

**A letter from Tokugawa Ieyasu granting lands to Yamamoto Jusaemon. 1582.**

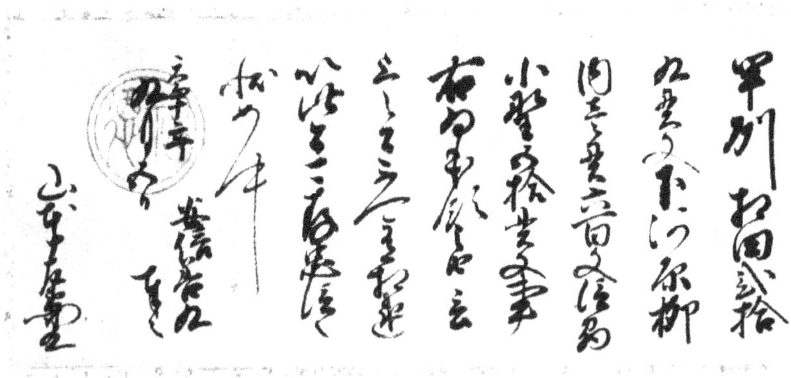

甲州相田弐拾
九貫文・下河原柳
内壱貫六百文・信州
小野五十貫文事、
右為本領之由言
上之間、不可有 相違、
以此旨可存忠信之
状如件、 天正十年
安倍善九 九月五日
（「福徳」朱印）奉之
山本十左衛門尉殿

Land worth twenty-nine Kan in the Aida area of Koshu. In the Shimohara Yanagi land worth One Kan and Six hundred Bun (One Bun is 1/1000th of a Kan). In the Ono area of Shinshu land worth Fifty Kan.

The regions mentioned to the right are declared under your control.

Let no person disagree with this.

That is all, yours in faith.

End of details regarding this award.

Tenth Year of Tensei

September Fifth

Lord Yamamoto Jusaemon

# The Kyo School of Sword

# Research into the Martial Art of Yamamoto Kansuke

## Regarding Yamamoto Kansuke's Kyo Ryu Kenjutsu

### 皇国剣道史

**Excerpts from: *History of Kendo in the Imperial Land***
**By Ozawa Aijiro**
**1944**

◇京　流

京流は鞍馬流とも稱し、源義家が、鞍馬山にて修行し神妙の劍法に達せし流れを酌みしものにて、山本勘助が最も有名である。勘助は諸國を修行し、後甲州に至り武田信玄に仕官し、足輕大將となり、武道指南に當つたが、元來勘助は、文武兩道に長じ、武具要說、並に百目錄等を書いて、信玄に奉つた。

當時の文獻に

「山本勘助文武ニ長ジ六韜三略ニ通ジ軍將タルノ人像ナリ、初メ今川義元ニ仕ヘントシ義元ニ謁見シタルニ、義元勘助ノ容貌甚ダ醜クカリシヲ見テ（ビツコ、片眼）輕侮ノ狀アリ勘助怒リテ去リ後武田信玄ニ重用セラル。」

とある。

又曰く京流は、鬼一法眼が、鞍馬の僧八人に傳へし、劍流の一つである。然し確たる文献なく、唯京流の劍士に、山本勘助、古岡憲法、荒井治部少輔、方波見備前等有名である。

## Kyo Ryu

Kyo Ryu is often referred to as Kurama Ryu. The household of Minomoto no Yoshitsune did Shugyo, or intensive training, at Mt. Kurama and was able to create a sublime style of sword fighting methodology. Probably Yamamoto Kansuke is the most famous disciple to drink in this flow and master it. Kansuke travelled all over Japan doing Shugyo, eventually ending up in Koshu where he served the General Takeda Shingen. There he became the commander of the Ashigaru "light foot" troops and was designated as the official instructor of martial arts. It is not often stated but Kansuke was adept not only at martial arts but also at learning. He wrote books on armaments as well as other military matters and presented them to General Shingen.

A document from that time contains the following passage,

*"Yamamoto Kansuke was adept at both military matters as well as wrote learning. By making use of the (military treatise) Rokuto Sanryaku he demonstrated what the ideal military leader should be like. The first time he was to offer his services to Imagawa Yoshimoto, Yoshimoto took one look at his appearance and recoiled. Due to his ugly appearance (lame in one leg, missing an eye) he was scornful. Kansuke, angered at this, left and later served with Takeda Shingen who greatly valued him."*

Further, legend sayeth that Kyo Ryu is a sword school descended from the eight Kurama monks that Kiichi Hogan taught. That being said there is no documentation confirming this to be found. All that remains is the famous followers of Kyo Ryu, the sword masters Yamamoto Kansuke, Yoshioka Kenpo, Arai Jibu Shoyu, and Katabami of Bizen.

文献によれば、吉岡憲法は、室町の師範となり、俗に兵法所と言はれた、代々足利将軍に仕へ武を以つて家憲となした、吉岡直賢の代に至り子二人あり、兄を源左衛門直綱、弟を又市郎直重といつた。宮本武蔵と立合つたのは兄源左衛門である。共に秀れたる武藝者であつた。又曰く源義経が鞍馬に於て劍を學び、其の門下に俊乗坊重源あり、其の弟子に達人八人あつた、之れが各門戸を張り世に鞍馬八流と稱せられたと。

齋藤判官傳鬼坊は、京都に於て妙技を天覽に供し、賞嘆の御勅を賜り有名である。居合で高名を馳せしは、奥州の林崎勘助重信、中興の祖と稱せられ、槍術では大和の寶藏院流の開祖、寶藏院胤榮、奥州の大内無邊、越前の富田牛生等有名であつた。

According to the records that do exist, Yoshioka Kenpo was a Shihan, or head instructor, to the Muromachi Shogun and his residence was generally known as a place one could learn martial arts. Generation after generation served the Ashikaga Shogun and the family name became synonymous with martial arts. In the generation of Yoshioka Naokata, there were two children. The eldest was called Gensaemon Naotsuna and the younger was called Mata Ichiro Naoshige. The one who fought Miyamoto Musashi was the elder brother Gensaemon. Both of them were experts at martial arts.

Also it is said that Minomoto Yoshitsune studied the sword at Kurama along with another disciple by the name of Junjobo Chogen. There were eight disciples that mastered this school and they spread out to various families and the art they taught became known as Kurama Hachi Ryu, the School of the Eight from Horse Saddle Mountain. Saito Hankan Denkibo became famous for the acclaim he received from the emperor for his presentation of sublime techniques in Kyoto. The man who became renowned for his Iai, or sword drawing technique, was Hayashizaki Kanjyo Shigenobu of Oshu. He is thought of as the father that reinvigorated the school.

As for Sojutsu, or spear techniques, there is the founder of the Hozoin School, Hozoin Inei. Other famous spear practitioners were Ouchi Mubei in Oshu and Toda Gyusho of Echizen, as well as others.

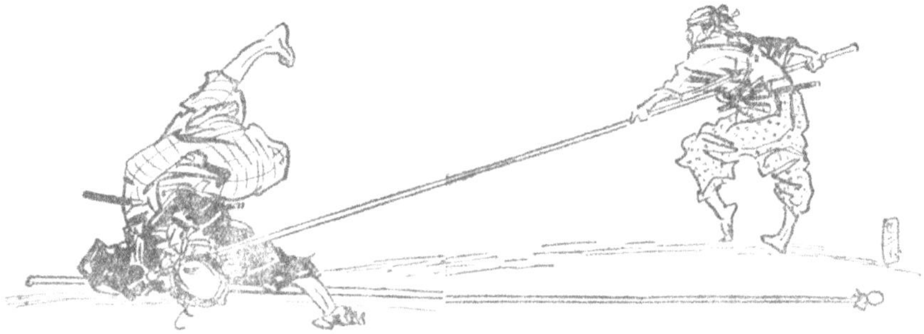

*Yamamoto Kansuke taking down Matsuta Shichiro Saemon in a spear fight*
Illustration from the Illustrated Koyo Gunkan by Matsuyama Shisui 1922.

# 第三章　京八流と關東七流

而して玆に見逃すべからざるは、源義經の神技に達せし、武法の流れを汲んだ一派がある。義經は頼朝の疑惑を買つて、陸奥に流れ、慘たる最後を遂げたが、鞍馬山にて鍛へし、武法は埋るべくもなく、其の遺鍊を受け其の流れを汲んだ達人が八人あつた、之れ等は京に於て武道の途を繼承し、よく世に弘めた。之れを京八流、又は鞍馬八流と稱した。

一方、上代に緒を發した、鹿島の太刀は、上古流、中古流の新舊二派に分れ、盛んに劍法を競ひ、武道の向上に貢したが、其の中、達人が七名あつた。世に之れを關東七流と稱し、京八流と對稱したのであつた。（其節參照）

## Chapter Three: Kyo Hachi Ryu and the Kanto Shichi Ryu
## The Eight Schools of Kyoto and the Seven Schools of the Kanto Region

It would be unforgivable to neglect to mention the school that drank in the flow derived from the supremely refined sword techniques of Minamoto Yoshitsune. Yoshitsune drew the suspicion of the Kamakura Shogun Yoritomo (his brother) and was sent off to Rikuoku. He was, in the end, able to turn his failure around and succeed. Realizing that the result of his extensive training at Kurama Mountains should not be buried and lost, he bequeathed his knowledge to eight disciples. These eight thoroughly drank in the flow this school and became experts. The tradition of training these martial arts continued under their guidance in Kyoto and later spread throughout Japan.

This school became known as Kyo Hachi Ryu, or the Kyoto Eight School. It was also referred to as Kurama Hachi Ryu, or the Eight of Kurama Mountain School.

On the other hand we have the Tachi style of Kashima, the thread of which began in ancient times. It is divided between the Upper Old Style and the Middle Old Style in a kind of Old School and New School. The both trained and competed to elevate the level of their sword technique above the other. In the process they contributed to the development of martial arts as a whole. Amongst them there were seven that stood out. They became known as the Kanto Shichi Ryu, or the Seven from Kanto School, and were often mentioned in contrast to the Kyoto Eight School.

# 第八章 劍法の型

劍法の型は、上代、日本武尊の三位、仁德帝時代の神妙劍、平安朝時代の五位等を擧げる事が出來るが、その內容に至つては、何等傳つてゐない。足利時代に於ても秘傳が多く、今日公開せらるゝものは、多くは後人が時代と共に改作したるものと見るべく、眞に開祖時代の型其のものを傳ふるとは信ずる事が出來ない。

幸にも、戰國時代に於ける、愛州移香の、陰流、山本勘助の京流の型が、其の當時の傳書に依つて知る事を得た。以つて足利末期の代表型として、參考とすべく、又其れ以前の型をも推測する事が出來る。（因に型は後に形と書くやうになつた）

## Chapter Eight: Kenpo no Kata
## The Stances of the Way of the Sword

From days long past The Stances of the Way of the Sword have existed. In the days of Yamato Takeru (72-114 CE) there were the Three Stances, in the era of the Tentoku Emperor (313-399) there was Shinmyo Ken, the Heavenly Mystery Sword and in the Heian Era there were the Five Stances and so on. While we can rattle off these names, today there is nothing that remains of these teachings.

There are a great number of secret teachings from the Ashikaga Era (1336-1573) however as those that are seen in public today were altered or completely replaced by later generations they should be viewed as such. The Kata, or Stances, presented now cannot be seen as true representations of what the original founders of the school made.

Fortunately for us, Densho from the Warring States Era of Yamamoto Kansuke's Kyo Ryu and Aisu Iko's Kage Ryu can show us something of the original. Through these we marvelous examples of Kata from the Late Ashikaga Era we can hypothesize what earlier Kata may have been like. Thus the Kanji used for Kata changed from 型 "shape" to 形 "form."

Translator's Note:

This book also reprints pages of Yamamoto Kansuke's *Sword Scroll*. The illustration below is labeled "Kyo Ryu Kamae" or (Sword) Stances of the Kyo School. It is not clear if the author called it Kyo Ryu because the book is attributed to Yamamoto Kansuke or he had other information.

“Kyo Ryu Kamae” Sword Stances of the Kyo School.

There is also this mysterious castle drawing with two figures sitting in a courtyard underneath the final archer versus spearman illustration. The author did not indicate from whence this edition of Kansuke's book came.

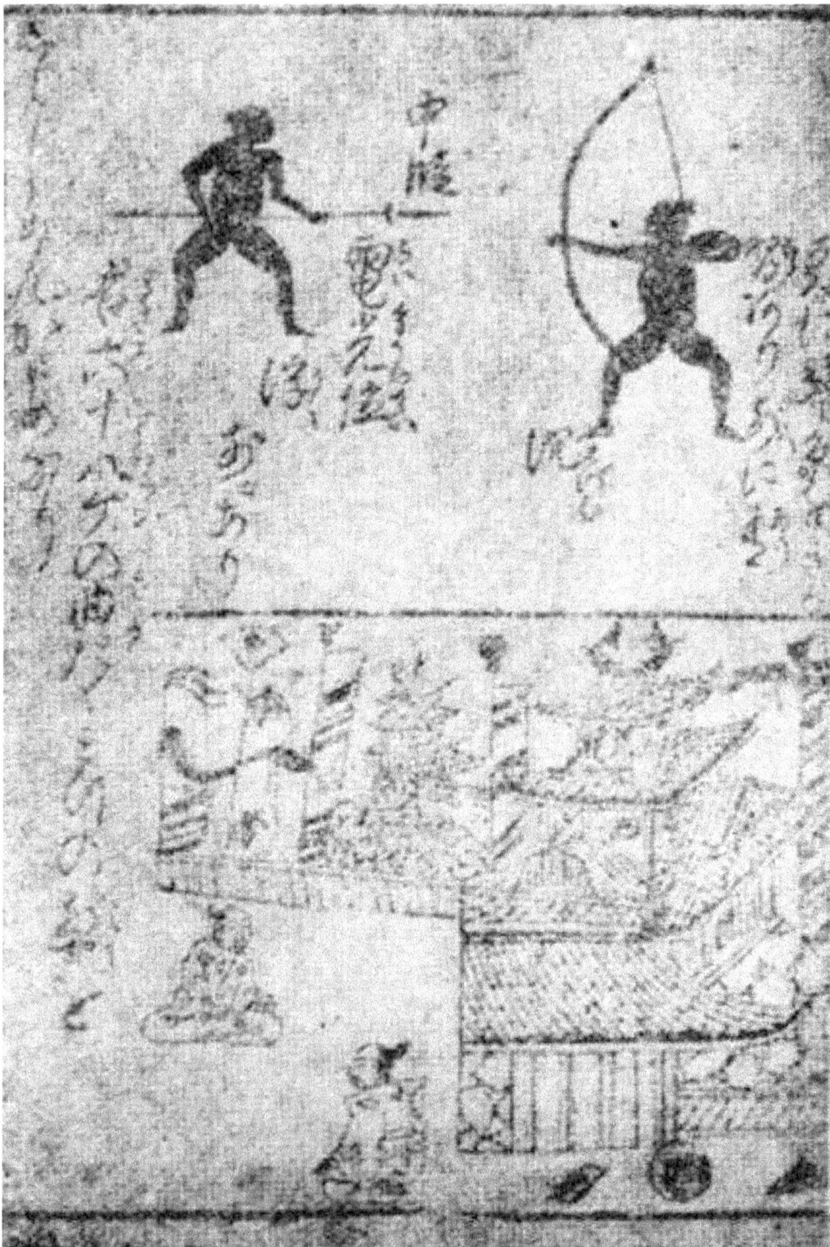

**From the *Encyclopedia of Martial Arts Schools***
**By Watatani Kiyoshi and Yamada Tadachika**
1963

## Kiichi Hogan Ryu

### A Military Strategy and Sword Fighting School
### Also Known as Kiichi Ryu
### From the Kouji Era (1555-1558)

The Sorcerer (Inyoshi) known as Hogen who lived in the Horikaa Ichijo section of Kyoto was a man who was an expert in both literary and martial arts. The story of Ushiwaka Maru, Minamoto no Yoshitsune's boyhood name, becoming familiar with the youngest daughter of Kiichi and using that relationship to steal a copy of the Chinese book of Military strategy known as Rikuto is nothing more than a legend drafted for the book *The Record of Yoshitsune*. It is unclear what part of this Ryu contains the direct teachings of Kiichi.

Returning to the beginning, his name was Kenkai, but he was also known as Imadegawa Yoshimaru from Yoshioka village in Iyo no Kuni, present day Shikoku. He was the grandchild of the son of Yoshioka Nobukiyo, the third generation Kenjo Ritsushi ( A kind of officer in charge of defense both military and magical). He was a student of the sorcerer scientist Abe. The story that he begged a copy of the *Rikuto San Ryaku* from Zaifu and became a master military tactician seems to be stretching the truth a bit. References can be found to a Provincial administrator named Kiichi (albeit with different Kanji) in the five volume *Narubehi* by Ogyu Sorai (1736), the *Towazugatari* by Shinosagi Tokai (Mid Edo) and in other books, but it is impossible to determine if this is the Kiichi in question.

It was during the era of Emperor Daigo that Oe no Koretoki made his way to China and returned with a copy of *Rikuto San Ryaku*. He translated it into Japanese and called it the Kinetsushu. That particular volume was passed on to the Ogasawara Clan. Another volume was brought over from China by Yoshibu Shubi and Kept at Kuramaji Temple.

Later in the era of the Shirakawa Emperor (1073-1087) Kiichi Hogan was able to get his hands on this copy. The story from the

*Bugei Shoden*, or *Short Transmissions of Martial Arts*, that relays the tale of Ushiwaka Maru secretly copying the volume is entirely a fabrication. In a Densho left by Jingo Izu no Kami, one of the top students of Kami Izumi Ise no Kami, it says that Yoshitsune bequeathed a Kuruma Ryu Densho to Shimogamo Temple.

That Jingo was able to gain access to this Densho through a spiritual dream is something of a jewel in the cup of this school. According to popular myth, Yoshitsune was able to steal a document called the Tora no Maki, or the *Tiger Scroll*, from Kiichi. This secret document was still being passed around through the end of the Edo Era, despite the fact that when and by whom this document was crafted is unclear. *The Tiger Scroll* primarily contains secret Shingon teachings of Jujutsu, or cursing techniques. The lineage of transmission extends in a winding and undulating fashion from when it was written during the reign of the Chinese Emperor Kosekiko (292-195 BCE) until it ends with Nishikawa Shinbei of Bunka (1800-1818) Era Edo. All around a wildly unusual situation.

At any rate, Kiichi is said to have taught the inner secrets of Kenjutsu to eight monks at Kurama Temple which, in turn, gave birth to the name Kyo no Hachi Ryu. Kyo refers to the city Kyoto and Hachi to the eight disciples.

Kaibara Ekiken (1630-1714) wrote in his book *Chiyaku* that Ushiwaka Maru was one of the original eight Kyo Ryu disciples.

## 京流

一、京流は古の京八流の一なりと云ひ、近來佐々木六角家の家人、荒井治部少輔此流に達し、後小田原北條家に仕へ世に名あり。又山本勘介入道道鬼も此流に達したりと云ふ。

## 道鬼流

一、道鬼流と稱し、山本勘介を祖として傳ふるもの、往々之あり。親しく聞きしは讃岐高松に富永甚兵衛あり。

## Excerpt from:
## *Gekken Sodan* 撃剣叢談
## by Mikami Genryu 1790

### Kyo Ryu
### Toki Ryu

- Kyo Ryu is said to originally be part of Kyo Hachi Ryu. Of late a member of the Sasaki Rokkaku household by the name of Arai Jibu Shoyu became expert at this school. Later he served Odawara Hojo and became renowned. It is also said that Yamamoto Kansuke Toki became highly skilled at this school. (Toki "Way of the Devil" is one of Kansuke's names)
- This school is often referred to as Toki Ryu with Yamamoto Kansuke being the founder. For detailed information about this, you should inquire with Tominaga Kanbei of the Takamatsu Domain of Kinuki Province.

川中島大合戦 1887 綱島亀吉

1887 Illustration showing the death of Yamamoto Kansuke at the Battle of Kawanaka Jima. By Tsunashima Kamekichi.

**Excerpts from:**
***Secrets of the Kyo Hachi School*** **秘伝京八流**
**by Watanabe Masatoshi 渡辺勝利**

京八流

京八流は、剣術の源流・始祖とされる流派の一つ。平安時代末期に鬼一法眼が京都の鞍馬山で 8 人の僧侶に刀法を伝えたところを始祖として、多くの剣術の源流となったとされる。しかしながら京八流に関する文献は室町期以降ほぼ消失しており、現代ではその実態を掴む事は難しい。源義経が師事した流派という伝説もあり、様々な人物伝や伝記などの伝承がある。

**Kyo Hachi Ryu**

Kyo Hachi Ryu is thought of as the source of Kenjutsu in Japan, one of the original schools of sword. At the end of the Heian Era, Kiichi Hogan taught Kenpo, the way of the sword, to eight monks at Mt. Kurama in Kyoto. After that the teachings spread and morphed into different schools. Unfortunately, most records relating to this Ryu were lost in the following Muromachi Era, thus it is hard to confirm any of this in the present day.

源義経

　源義経は京に生まれ、幼少期に鞍馬寺において剣術を学んだとされる。この義経が学んだ流派が京八流、またはその一派ではないかと言われる。義経の剣術は「敏捷性を生かし、短い刀を用いて素早く敵の懐に入る剣術」だったとされ、義経が源平合戦において実際に使用したとされる車太刀は短く

**Minamoto no Yoshitsune**

Minamoto no Yoshitsune, who was born in Kyoto, is said to have studied Kenjutsu at Kurama Temple. It is said that he either studied Kyo Hachi Ryu or a derivation of that school. Yoshitsune described his Kenjutsu as, "Focused on bringing out the nimbleness of the sword. This Kenjutsu uses a short Katana to move deep inside the enemy's guard." The type of sword Yoshitsune actually used in the Genpei War was called a Kurama Gatana and it is still at Kurama Dera Temple in Kyoto.

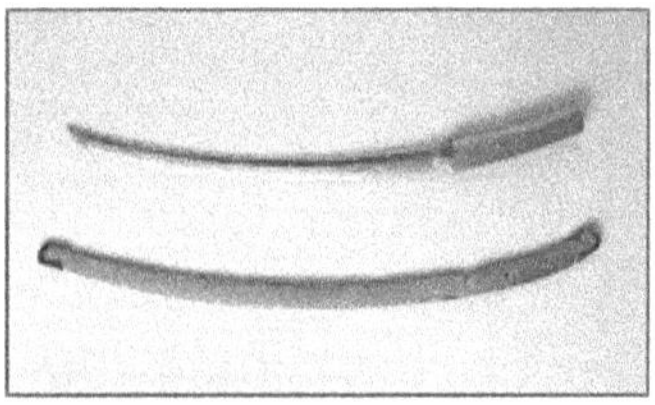

## 京流

「山本勘助」は武田信玄に仕えた軍師であるが、彼の使った剣術・兵法は「京流」とされている。これが京八流であるかは定かでは無いが彼の剣技の腕前については次のような記述がある
「天文 17 年(1548)に南部下野守が家臣の石井藤三郎を成敗しようとして失敗。この藤三郎を勘助が心張り棒を使って倒し下野守に引き渡した。」 -甲陽軍鑑
おそらく新当流を修め、かつ真剣を持った藤三郎を棒で倒した技術は見事であり、逸話が事実ならこの「京流」は優れた剣術であった事が分かる。また、同じく甲斐国の武田信玄に仕えた軍師「前原筑前守」も「京流」の達人とされる。
「上野先方侍である前原筑前守は剣術・京流の達人で、投げられた複数の扇子を続けざまに切り落とすなど優れた剣の腕を持つ」 - 本朝武芸小伝
これらの文献には「京流」が明確に登場しているが、この「京流」は「京八流」の一派なのか京の剣術全般の事を指しているのかは定かでは無い。

## Kyo Ryu

Yamamoto Kansuke was a military tactician on the side of Takeda Shingen and was said to have used Kyo Ryu military science and sword fighting, but it is not possible to verify whether his school of war was Kyo Ryu or not. We do have the following quote establishing Kansuke's skill as a swordsman.

*"In Tenmon 7 (1548) Nambu Shimotsuke Mamori failed in his attempt to gain a victory for his retainer Ishii Fujisaburo. Kansuke took Fujisaburo down with a Shinbai-bo, a utilitarian stick used to prevent a sliding window from being opened, and returned him beaten to Shimotsuke Mamori."* –Koyo Gunkan

This gives us a glimpse of Kansuke's prowess with the sword. Despite the fact that Fuji Saburo, a practitioner of Shinto Ryu, was armed with a Katana Kansuke was able to defeat him with a stick.

In the Honcho Bugei Shoden, or *Japanese Short Tales of Martial Arts*, it says,

*"A Samurai of Ueno by the name of Maebara Tsukumae Mamori was an expert at Kyo Ryu Kenjutsu. You could continuously throw any number of folding fans at him and his prowess was such that they would all be cut down."*

The name of the sword school Kyo Ryu can be clearly seen in this passage. Whether this Kyo Ryu is the same as Kyo Hachi Ryu or it simply refers to a type of Kenjutsu originating in Kyoto is unclear.

吉岡流

吉岡憲法直元が創始した吉岡流も京八流の末流という説がある、吉岡流の剣士としては江戸時代初期に宮本武蔵と争った吉岡清十郎、吉岡伝七郎が有名であるが、当の吉岡一門が断絶しており、文献が残されていない。

**Yoshioka Ryu**

There is some evidence that Yoshioka Kenpo's Yoshioka Ryu has a connection to Kyo Hachi Ryu. As the entire school was decimated by Miayamo Musashi no confirmation of this can be made.

上記のように京八流及びその系譜とされる剣術の殆どは近世以降失伝しているが、「剣術の源流」「始祖が鬼一法眼」という京八流の伝承は広く親しまれており、現代に至るまでさまざまな演劇や文学作品、漫画作品などの設定に用いられている。

As can be seen by what is written above, most branches of Kyo Hachi Ryu have become lost beginning in the modern Era. Kyo Ryu is widely thought of as, "The Source of Kenjutsu," while Kiichi Hogen is thought of as, "The Founding Father of Kenjutsu." These concepts feature in many modern-day plays, literature and manga.

www.ingramcontent.com/pod-product-compliance
Lightning Source LLC
Chambersburg PA
CBHW020005290326
41935CB00007B/315
*9781950959242*